The Semantic Basis of
Argument Structure

DISSERTATIONS IN LINGUISTICS

A series edited by
Joan Bresnan, Sharon Inkelas, William J. Poser, and Peter Sells

The aim of this series is to make work of substantial empirical breadth and theoretical interest available to a wide audience.

The Semantic Basis of Argument Structure

STEPHEN WECHSLER

WITHDRAWN

CSLI Publications
Center for the Study of Language and Information
Stanford, California

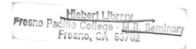

Library of Congress Cataloging-in-Publication Data
Wechsler, Stephen 1956–
    The semantic basis of argument structure : a study of the relation between
    word meaning and syntax / Stephen Wechsler.
    p. cm. — (Dissertations in linguistics series)
    Chiefly a revision of the author's thesis (doctoral—Stanford, 1991).
    Includes bibliographical references and index.

    ISBN 1–881526–69–0 (cloth)
    ISBN 1–881526–68–2 (paper)
    1. Semantics. 2. Grammar, Comparative and general— Syntax. 3. Order
    (Grammar) 4. Grammar, Comparative and general— Complement
    I. Title. II. Series: Dissertations in linguistics.
    P325.W36 1995
    401'.43—dc20   95–14885
                                             CIP

"Papier peint. Applications d'etoffes et broderie Eucalyptus (Fig. 306)," the drawing on the cover of the paperback edition of this book is by Maurice-Pillard Verneuil from his *Étude de la Plante: Son application aux industries d'art* (1903, Paris: Librairie centrale des beaux-arts). Courtesy Richard Manuck.

∞ The acid-free paper used in this book meets the minimum requirments of the American National Standard for Information Sciences—Permanence of Paper for Printed Library Materials, ANSI Z39.48-1984.

Contents

Preface

The first three chapters of this book consist of a revised version of my 1991 Stanford doctoral dissertation in linguistics. The dissertation was written during a period of increasing interest by syntacticians in the interface between syntax and word meaning. Four years later, this interest shows no sign of waning, as theories of thematic roles, lexical conceptual structures, and lexical decomposition continue to appear in the linguistics literature. These theories vary considerably both in their ontological richness, and in the range of linguistic phenomena they attempt to explain. In both respects, this book takes a rather parsimonious approach in its excursion to the borderlands of syntax, lexical semantics, and morphology. In the theory of word meaning presented here, the ontological 'provisions' for the journey are limited to a few semantic primitives for which I can find independent semantic justification. At the same time, I was able to pack light for this trip in part because the conception of lexical syntax adopted here has allowed me to limit the range of the journey. In other words, I have tried to keep the theory simple by not asking it to do more than what is necessary.

The fourth chapter, which was completed in 1995, introduces two new ideas. The first is an attempt to reformulate the theory within a 'hierarchical lexicon' of the sort proposed by Flickinger (1987), inter alia. This reformulation addresses the problem of treating certain lexical exceptions to the generalizations captured by the theory, and also eliminates the need for a rather stipulative preposition selection rule. The second proposal in chapter 4 provides a better developed theory of grammatical relations by revising the rules for mapping between roles and complements. In particular, this proposal is an attempt to capture the insight of Kiparsky (1987) that the mapping between thematic roles and grammatical relations is conditioned by parochial morphosyntactic properties of a language.

There are many people who helped at each stage of this project. The initial work on chapter 4 was made possible by a summer research award from University Research Institute at the University of Texas in Austin. For the dissertation itself, I had the privilege and good fortune of working with Paul Kiparsky, whose ideas in this area first sparked my interest and inspired me. My other committee members, Ivan Sag, Stanley

Peters, and Peter Sells also gave me invaluable help and guidance. Others who have discussed this work with me, at various stages, include Annie Zaenen, Bill Ladusaw, Henry Smith, Chris Piñon, Tony Davis, Paul Kroeger, Cleo Condoravdi, Stella Markantonatou, and Marc Verhagen. Also, I am grateful to Dikran Karagueuzian and Tony Gee for their roles in the publication of this book. Finally, I wish to thank Marie, for everything.

1

Introduction

1 Argument structure and linking

Central to an adequate theory of complementation is an account of the role of lexical semantics. Verbs subcategorize syntactically for complements and express semantically a relation having argument slots to be filled by the interpretations of these complements. Such lexical items need to specify in their lexical entry which argument slots are to be filled by (the interpretations of) which complements. For example in the interpretation of (1), the giver, recipient, and gift argument slots of the *DONATE* relation are filled by John, his books, and the library, respectively.

(1)   John donated his books to the library.

(2)   *DONATE*(giver: *John*,   recipient: *the.library*,   gift: *John's.books*)

The first question we will ask is this: What is the nature of the linguistic knowledge in virtue of which a speaker of English connects the state of affairs in (2) with the string of words in (1) rather than to any of the strings in (3), which fail to express the right meaning, or (4), which are ungrammatical?

(3)   a.   #The library donated John to his books.
       b.   #The library donated his books to John.
       c.   #John donated the library to his books.
       d.   #John donated his books from the library.

(4)   a.   *The library John his books donated.
       b.   *The library John his books to donated.

To start with, the syntactic complements are naturally thought of as linearly ordered in a subcategorization ('subcat') list representing a hierarchy of dependent elements ordered according to relative obliqueness, with the least oblique on the left (viz. SUBJECT < OBJECTS < OBLIQUES) (Sag 1985):

(5)   *donate*
      [SUBCAT   < NP, NP, PP[*to*] >]

Each verb's lexical entry includes a subcat set, specifying how many complements it takes and of what category; this set is linearly ordered to a subcat *list* by universal principles involving syntactic category (e.g. NPs are less oblique than PPs). This ordering influences the positions of those complements in phrase structure and other syntactic properties: roughly speaking, the left-most NP is the subject, the next NP is the object, and so on (see section 3 below for details).

I will adopt the view that the argument slots of the semantic content of such lexical items are also linearly ordered by universal principles, but of a semantic nature:

(6)   *donate*
$$\begin{bmatrix} \text{SUBCAT} & < \text{NP}, \text{NP}, \text{PP}[to] > \\ \text{ROLES} & < \text{giver:}\_\_, \text{recipient:}\_\_, \text{gift:}\_\_ > \end{bmatrix}$$

Roughly speaking, this ordering on roles reflects the so-called 'thematic prominence', as represented in thematic hierarchies (cp. Jackendoff 1972, Foley and Van Valin 1984), but eventually we will arrive at the ordering in a different way. The lexical entry specifies which argument slots are to be filled by (the interpretations of) which complements, indicated here by coindexing:

(7)   *donate*
$$\begin{bmatrix} \text{SUBCAT} & < \text{NP}_1, \text{NP}_3, \text{PP}[to]_2 > \\ \text{ROLES} & < \text{giver:}1, \text{recipient:}2, \text{gift:}3 > \end{bmatrix}$$

The interpretation of the noun phrase corresponding to NP_1 places a semantic restriction on the entity filling the giver slot, and so on for the other complements: if NP_1 is [John]$_{\text{NP}}$ then this restricts the filler of the giver slot to some individual named John. Thus (7) represents the linguistic knowledge we sought above.

This dissertation addresses two closely related questions. The first question concerns the nature of the universal and language-specific semantic constraints on *argument structure* (Williams 1981, Marantz 1984, Bresnan and Kanerva 1989, Grimshaw 1990), a representation including, for us, the ordering of roles plus certain other types of argument slot classification. Our second concern is *linking theory*, which deals with the universal and language-specific constraints on possible mappings between argument structures and subcategorization lists.

The theories of argument structure and linking are responsible for explaining, among other things, generalizations governing subject selection (Fillmore 1968), and, more generally, *argument selection.* The by now familiar observation is that languages follow certain systematic patterns regarding the expression of arguments as subjects and objects. For example, it is often noted that NPs denoting 'Agents' (causers, effectors, etc.) rarely if ever appear as objects with the subject NP denoting an entity affected by that Agent in virtue of the denoted action. Argument selection generalizations are purportedly universal, or at the very least they have strong cross-linguistic validity. It is unlikely that there is even a single language in the world where, in a sentence meaning 'Cooper ate the doughnut', the arguments are reversed so that 'Cooper' is the object and the NP denoting 'the doughnut' is the subject—where subjects have an independent status in the grammar motivated by construal relations such as control (control targets are subjects), raising (the raised NP is the subject) and anaphoric binding (some languages have subject-oriented reflexives). Beyond such gross generalizations, a web of subtler patterns can be detected.

This dissertation makes three basic claims, one about the nature of the semantic constraints on argument structure, one about semantically restricted linking, and a general universal principle of linking. These three claims are briefly summarized here; they will be explained and defended in detail in subsequent chapters.

(i) *Ordering rules.* The rules imposing the linear ordering on argument roles are universal and therefore are built from a universal primitive semantic basis. It has sometimes been suggested that this primitive basis includes a universal set of thematic role types such as Agent, Theme, and Goal (Fillmore 1968, *inter alia*) or a set of basic predicates such as CAUSE and GO out of which lexical semantic structures are made (Jackendoff 1990, *inter alia*). However, we hypothesize that the appropriate semantic basis involves primitives of an even more abstract and general sort, and that they are very few in number. Indeed there may only be one or two of them (see Chapter 2).

(ii) *Semantically restricted complements.* In addition there are certain more specific classifications of roles involving parochial language-specific semantic relations. A parochial semantic relation may appear in a rule of this kind only if it is associated with a formal element in the language which identifies a unique NP, such as an adposition or a semantic case-marker. For example, in the argument structure of *donate,* the second role (the 'recipient' role) is linked to the *to*-PP because the semantic contents of *donate* and *to* stand in the appropriate relation. But not all argument slots for every verb can 'find' a preposition (etc.) with the appropriate meaning; English *to* is available for the recipient role, but nothing is available for the *donor* and *gift* roles. Following Bresnan and Kanerva (1989), roles like the recipient will be called *restricted* roles ($[+r]$), while the donor and gift roles are unrestricted ($[-r]$), as indicated in (8).

(8)   *donate*
$$\left[\begin{array}{ll} \text{SUBCAT} & < NP_1, NP_3, PP[\textit{to}]_2 > \\ \text{ROLES} & < \text{giver}[-r]{:}1, \text{recipient}[+r]{:}2, \text{gift}[-r]{:}3 > \end{array}\right]$$

As a rule restricted roles must link to restricted complements with the appropriate semantics (cp. the restrictiveness constraint of Smith 1992).

(iii) *Isomorphy Condition.* The mapping between unrestricted roles and complements is an order isomorphism, i.e., lines of association between unrestricted roles and the complements filling them cannot cross. The linking shown in brackets violates this principle:

(9)   *Isomorphy Condition.*

$$*\left[\begin{array}{ll} \text{SUBCAT} & <...x_2...y_1...> \\ \text{ROLES} & <...[-r]{:}1...[-r]{:}2...> \end{array}\right]$$

But the linking of *donate* in (8) is not a violation, even though 2 precedes 3 on the roles list and follows on the subcat list, because 2's role is restricted ($[+r]$).

The Isomorphy Condition is motivated by the strong tendency for natural language to avoid alternations involving a reversal of the unrestricted complements such as subject and object NPs, while allowing reversals between complements if one or more indicates the semantic restriction on the role with a preposition, semantic case, or other marker of thematic role.[1] Subject-object reversals are rare, while alternations like *The acid dissolves metal/This metal dissolves in acid* are common. For example Chinese localizer affixes like *-shang* 'on' are normally optional but become obligatory in inversion constructions like (10) (Fu Tan, p.c.):

---

[1] An apparent exception occurs in passives of ditransitive applied verbs in 'symmetrical object' Bantu languages. These will not be treated here. See Bresnan and Moshi 1990.

(10) a.   xuesheng [zai   tai-**shang**] zuo   zhe.
              students   PREP   stage-**on**   sit   ASP.
              'The students are sitting on the stage.'

       b.   (zai)   tai-**shang** zuo zhe xuesheng
            (PREP) stage-**on** sit ASP students
            'On the stage are sitting the students.'

While the preposition *zai* is optional, the localizer *-shang* is obligatory in (10b). With verbs like *jin* 'enter' the localizer *-li* 'inside' is optional when the locative object appears in the normal uninverted construction (11a) but the localizer is obligatory in the inverted construction as shown in (11b).[2]

(11) a.   shui jin   le   wu(-**li**)
             water enter ASP house(-inside)
             'The water entered the house'

       b.   wu-**li**   jin le   shui
            house-inside enter ASP water
            'The water entered the house'

       c.   *wu   jin le   shui
            house enter ASP water

See Tan 1991 for evidence that the preposed locative in (11b) is the subject. Crucially this subject-object inversion can occur only when a locative marker (*-li*) appears to indicate explicitly that 'house' is restricted to the locative role.

    This parallels the behavior of optionally transitive English verbs like *pierce, reach,* or *penetrate,* as in the following:

---

[2]A small group of Chinese verbs allow omission of the localizer even in the inversion construction. An example is *zhong* 'shoot':

(i)   zidan zhong le   lao Li de zuo tui.
             bullet shoot ASP Mr. Li DE left leg
            'The bullet shot Mr. Li's left leg.'

(ii)   Lao Li de zuo tui zhong le   zidan
            Mr. Li DE left leg shoot ASP bullet

(12) a.   The needle pierced (through) the cushion.
      b.   Through the cushion pierced the needle.
      c.   *The cushion pierced the needle.

(13) a.   The boy reached (into) the lake.
      b.   Into the lake reached the boy.
      c.   (*)The lake reached the boy.

(12c) lacks the reading synonymous with (12a) and has only a strange, implausible one. Alternations which reverse two unrestricted roles, such as (12c) and (13c) are ruled out by the Isomorphy Constraint since the lines of association would have to cross for one of the two alternants.

Let us leave aside linking for now and consider some difficult problems one faces in arriving at semantic constraints on argument structure. While the ordering of the ROLES list is a feature of verbs, our sole access to semantic intuitions about verbs is through entire utterances in context. The sort of 'role' played by a participant in a situation as described by an utterance depends on innumerable factors including adverbial modifiers, the nature of the individuals filling the roles, and so on. To take one example of a sort that can be duplicated ad infinitum, the individual denoted by the subject of *save* plays a very different role in these two situations, even though the verb seems to have the same sense:

(14) a.   Fred saved the tulips from certain death (by watering them).
      b.   The dike saved the tulips from certain death (when the water level rose).

Fred is a cognitive agent who carries out a certain plan of action which brings it about that the tulips survive; but in the situation described by (14b) the dike is about as non-agentive as one can imagine: it quite literally does nothing whatsoever. Instead its presence simply becomes relevant to the tulips' fate whenever the water rises above grade.

This propensity for the semantic roles of participants to depend upon so many factors beyond the lexicosemantics of the verb makes the job of stating precise role ordering rules difficult, but not impossible. The key, I believe, is not to seek semantic primitives which are vague enough that our intuitions may be stretched to cover a wide range of situations, but rather to seek primitives which are precise and about which intuitions are firm, but which are common denominators over a wide range of situations. The next section reviews the literature on argument structure and various alternatives which have been proposed. The primary problem which emerges from that discussion is that of ascertaining and justifying the primitive semantic basis for this theory.

2 Previous approaches to argument structure

A great deal of study of the relation between lexicosemantics and morphosyntax across diverse languages has yielded extremely robust argument selection generalizations which cannot be due to coincidence and clearly deserve explanation. A variety of concrete proposals have been made for capturing these generalizations within a theory of grammar, some of which will be summarized below. Although the generalizations in question govern the relation between syntax and lexical semantics, previous theories have tended to stress the syntactic side and vary considerably in how explicit and detailed an account of lexical semantics they include.

The frameworks for studying this problem can be roughly divided into *thematic role* approaches and *lexical decomposition* approaches depending on the sort of semantic primitives they employ. Thematic role approaches assume a universal set of discrete thematic role types like AGENT, THEME, and RECIPIENT, while the lexical decomposition approaches assume a universal set of functions like GO, CAUSE, and BECOME. Some theories combine the two (e.g. Foley and Van Valin 1984). In addition there are some subtle variants of each of these which we will review below.

2.1 Thematic roles types

The basic idea behind thematic role theories is to classify the arguments of a verb according to the 'role' which the participants corresponding to those arguments play in the situation described by the clause in question. For example, in a sentence like *John gave his dog a bone*, 'John' might be classified as playing the Agent role since he brings about the event; 'his dog' might be classified as playing the Recipient role since it receives something (a bone) in virtue of the action; and 'a bone' is typically classified as a Theme, the classification given to participants which undergo a change of possession, location, etc.

Accordingly, we might say that the three argument slots of the particular verb *give* are classified into the equivalence classes Agent, Recipient, and Theme. Once classified in this manner, rules or constraints are given for mapping these argument slots onto the syntax. One may proceed by mapping first to grammatical functions like SUBJECT and OBJECT (or features thereof as in Bresnan and Kanerva 1989) or mapping to positions in d-structure (as in Baker 1988), or various other means. But in all thematic role theories the ultimate goal is to define a mapping between the set of argument slots of a verb, as classified into thematic role types, to the morphosyntactic 'addresses' for the complements filling those slots, within the clause (semantically) headed by the verb.

Typically this mapping is defined in some combination of absolute and relativistic terms. Absolute rules taking the form 'Agents cannot be mapped to syntactic objects' or 'Agents cannot be mapped to NPs dominated by VP at D-structure' have been proposed within the framework of Lexical Mapping Theory (LMT; Bresnan and Kanerva 1989) and many versions of Government/Binding theory (GB; Chomsky 1981), according to which certain roles (roughly the Agents) are said to be *external arguments* (Williams 1981), which appear external to the maximal projection of the verb (VP) at d-structure.

For relativistic rules such theories usually invoke a thematic hierarchy like the following to determine argument selection (Jackendoff 1972, Foley and Van Valin 1984, Bresnan and Kanerva 1989, Kiparsky 1987):

(15)   Agent < Instrument < Recipient/Experiencer < Theme < Location

The idea is that for the set of roles assigned by any given predicator, the highest (=leftmost) role on this hierarchy is mapped to the subject grammatical function. Thus in an argument set containing an Agent and a Theme, the Agent is mapped to the subject and the Theme to the object, because Agent is higher than Theme on this hierarchy.

Researchers also cite independent generalizations converging on the thematic hierarchy. In languages like German with relatively free complement order the default or discourse-neutral order follows the hierarchy: Agents precede Themes, Themes precede Locatives, and so on (Uszkoreit 1987). Idioms have a strong preference for including lower roles while leaving a higher role as the free position in the idiom (Kiparsky 1987). Thus Verb+Locative idioms are very common (*throw X to the wolves, bring X to light*, etc.), as are Verb+Theme idioms (*give X a hand, show X the door*, etc), and even V+Theme+Locative idioms (*bring home the bacon, let the cat out of the bag,* etc.) but V+Theme+Recipient idioms are rare (*give the devil his due*) and other combinations involving higher roles (Verb+Recipient, Verb+Agent, Verb+Goal+Agent, etc.) are very scarce, especially when the free position is lower on the hierarchy (one example is *the devil take X!*).[3]   Essentially the same tendency emerges in patterns of noun incorporation in those languages allowing it. Lower roles tend to

---

[3]All of these examples are from Kiparsky 1987:36. See Nunberg et al 1994 for a critique of this argument from idiom patterning.

incorporate more freely, leaving higher roles to be expressed in the usual analytic manner, while the converse is dispreferred (Mithun 1984). Kiparsky (1987) represents the thematic hierarchy not in terms of relative prominence but of semantic constituency, where the lower roles are 'closer' to the verb:

(16) < Agent < Instrument < Rec/Exp < Theme < Location *verb* >>>>>

When the thematic hierarchy is looked at this way, the patterns of idiom-formation and noun-incorporation can be seen as reflecting a tendency for 'semantic constituents' to be lexicalized.

Thematic role theories vary greatly in such matters as what the proper set of thematic roles is (e.g. some distinguish between Patient and Theme), what the precise ordering of the thematic hierarchy should be (e.g. some place Location above Theme), and so on. Most such theories implicitly involve a system of cross-classification across different semantic domains or 'fields', and in theories such as Ostler 1979 this is made explicit. At various points later in this dissertation we will return to such issues of detail, but first I would like to look at some more basic issues faced by all theories.

2.2 The semantics of discrete thematic roles

First consider the question of identifying thematic roles: How do we know when a given argument of a verb belongs to a particular thematic role class? That is, how do we know an Agent (Theme, etc.) when we see one? What sort of semantic criteria should be applied? How strictly should they be applied?

Dowty (1986) considers, and ultimately rejects, the possibility that thematic roles can be identified on the basis of lexical entailments. His discussion also introduces some useful terminology into this area. First an *ordered argument system* is distinguished from a true *thematic role system*. An ordered argument system is simply a scheme for distinguishing between the arguments of a verb, but in actual practice linguists often use labels such as Agent and Patient as a way of suggesting which argument they have in mind. The two arguments of *bake*, the baker and thing-baked, might be informally referred to as the Agent and Theme respectively. Such labels are not meant to have any semantic content, nor to serve as equivalence classes across semantic roles. When we begin to develop explicit analyses in Chapter 2 of this dissertation, we will not assume a thematic role system; labels such as Agent and Theme will be used only in this informal manner, for identifying arguments, except of course in commentary on thematic role systems in other theories.[4]

In order to arrive at a definition of the kind of thematic role with semantic content, Dowty (1986) first defines an *individual thematic role* as follows:

(17) Given an n-place predicate δ and a particular argument x_i, the *individual thematic role* $<\delta, i>$ is the set of all properties α such that the entailment $\Box[\delta(x_1, \ldots x_i, \ldots x_n) \rightarrow \alpha(x_i)]$ holds.

The individual thematic role represents semantic information specific to a particular argument slot of a particular verb: e.g. the 'builder' individual thematic role of the verb *build* includes every property knowable about x on the basis of knowing that the sentence 'x builds y' is true.

Building on individual thematic roles, Dowty defines a *thematic role type* as follows:

(18) Given a set T of pairs $<\delta, i_\delta>$, where δ is an n-place predicate and i_δ the index of one of its arguments, a *thematic role type* τ is the intersection of all the individual thematic roles determined by T.

For example, let T = {< hit, hitter >, < kill, killer >, <devour, devourer>}. The *individual* thematic role for the 'hitter' argument is the set of properties entailed to hold of that argument by virtue of it being that particular argument of *hit*, and so on for the other verbs. The thematic role *type* for T is the intersection of these three sets of properties.

Such an intersection of properties can in principle be calculated for any random assemblage of individual thematic roles. But the question of interest to linguists is whether there exist special thematic role types like 'Agent' and 'Patient' which are relevant to linguistic theory. These distinguished sets Dowty calls *L-Thematic Role Types*, or simply Thematic Roles. The empirical question which he (like many others) considers is whether L-Thematic Role Types exist. For example, is there some set of entailments shared by all 'Agents' and no 'non-Agents'? By Agent here we

---

[4]Morphosyntactic forms with semantic content, such as semantic (oblique) cases and adpositions, may be said to mark a particular thematic role type: Dative marks Recipients, and so on. Thus Dative case in a particular language marks a language internal equivalence class, if you will, but this need not be a cross-linguistic class, nor a universal semantic primitive. Its status is similar to that of other lexical items with semantic content. See Chapter 3 below.

mean some set of roles which is relevant to our syntactic mapping rules. This same question can be asked for all such thematic role 'labels' which we mention in our linking rules.

Dowty (1986) concludes that L-thematic Role Types do not exist, that it does not seem to be possible to specify sets of entailments which pick out the desired notions Agent, Theme, etc. This seems particularly clear for the role Theme, which occurs in a wide variety of different verb types. But it is difficult and probably impossible to establish a set of criterial entailments even for relatively clear semantic notions such as Agenthood. Agents do not have to be volitional, for example (*The disease killed him*). Once we leave the realm of volition it becomes unclear that one can identify an individual object as a 'causer' of an event. The cause of the event described by *the acid dissolved the metal* is not the acid alone but a larger situation consisting of the acid and metal juxtaposed under the right conditions. See Chapter 2, section 2 below.

Dowty (1986:28-29) notes that 'there is surprisingly little consensus on what the set of linguistically significant role types is.' With respect to syntactic phenomena purportedly dependent on thematic role types such as Agent and Patient, the roles tend to fragment into distinct though closely-related types. One construction may require a 'Volitional' Agent, while another requires an 'Initiative' Agent, and so on. More importantly, he argues that when the semantic content of the roles is specified with precision, the system becomes incapable of explaining the syntactic phenomena which it is adduced to explain.

Nevertheless, we will later embrace a version of the entailment-based account. We will see that such an account is workable as long as the theory is not asked to do more than it needs to. In particular, we do not need to assume that all roles are classified into role types. Also, it turns out that the defining properties (α in (17) above) are primarily of a relational sort, that is, they involve coarguments of the predicate in question.

Before turning to our proposal, we will tentatively follow Dowty (1986) in concluding that this entailment-based approach is doomed. From that assumption, it still does not follow that thematic role systems are not feasible, since it might be that lexical entailments are not the right way of defining thematic role types. Next we consider some alternatives.

2.3 Proto-Roles and many-to-one mappings

Let us consider some of the alternatives which have been suggested. First of all, we can reject outright the idea that thematic roles should be identified by syntactic tests alone, without reference to semantics. The idea would be that arguments fall into classes according to their syntactic behavior, and terms like Agent and Theme are just labels for these classes.

My reason for rejecting this is not that such classes do not exist (in fact they do), but that such an approach cannot possibly solve the problem which we have set out to solve: to elucidate the relationship between morphosyntax and semantics.

A related suggestion is that arguments fall into syntactic classes, and then semantic notions are associated with these classes in a many-to-one fashion. I am aware of two versions of this idea. The first involves so-called *Proto-Roles* (Dowty 1991, Zaenen 1993).[5] The second involves associating argument classes with positions in lexical decompositions ('logical form', 'logical structure', etc.) (Foley and Van Valin 1984, Van Valin 1990). In this section we focus on the Proto-Role approach, then review lexical decomposition in the next section.

The idea behind the Proto-Role approach is that argument selection principles should not be described in terms of discrete roles. Rather, Dowty proposes that there are really only two thematic-role-like concepts involved in argument selection, and these are 'cluster concepts,' not discretely defined ones. He calls them the Agent Proto-Role and Patient Proto-Role. These are to be the (only) thematic categories on which linking principles are stated. These are the specific properties Dowty (1991:572) gives:

(19)   Contributing properties for the Agent Proto-Role:
        a.   volitional involvement in the event or state
        b.   sentience (and/or perception)
        c.   causing an event or change of state in another participant
        d.   movement (relative to the position of another participant)
        (e.   exists independently of the event named by the verb)

---

[5]Certain aspects of Foley and Van Valin's conception very closely anticipate Dowty's 1991 proto-roles proposal. What Foley and Van Valin call thematic roles, defined according to position in 'logical structure', have the same theoretical status as the 'prototypical properties' of Dowty's two proto-roles: for Foley and Van Valin they determine relative preferences for the two 'macro-roles' (Foley and Van Valin 1984:59). What Dowty called the Agent and Patient Proto-Roles, Foley and Van Valin called the Actor and Undergoer Macro-Roles, respectively.

(20)   Contributing properties for the Patient Proto-Role:
     a.   undergoes change of state
     b.   incremental theme[6]
     c.   causally affected by another participant
     d.   stationary relative to movement of another participant
    (e.   does not exist independently of the event, or not at all)

Dowty suggests that the Proto-Roles act as semantic defaults in the acquisition of lexical meaning. The idea is that the properties are 'prototypical', so that no single property is essential for either role. Instead, he gives the following procedure:

(21)   Argument selection principle: In predicates with grammatical subject and object, the argument for which the predicate entails the greatest number of Proto-Agent properties will be lexicalized as the subject of the predicate; the argument having the greatest number of Proto-Patient entailments will be lexicalized as the direct object. (Dowty 1991:576)

Notice that there is no attempt to find some unifying semantics behind the lists of properties in (19) and (20). Proto-Agent and Proto-Patient are 'cluster concepts' or 'higher-order generalizations about meanings' which map directly onto the syntax in accordance with (21).

Zaenen 1993 is an adaptation of the Proto-Role hypothesis to Lexical Mapping Theory (LMT; Bresnan and Kanerva 1989). Zaenen's analysis is interesting for several reasons, one being that it helps to clarify the status of thematic role labels like Agent and Theme as used in LMT. First I will briefly summarize the theory of LMT as described in most papers on it, including Bresnan and Kanerva 1989; then we will see how Zaenen's proposal fits in.

In LMT the two binary features r(estricted) and o(bjective) cross-classify the grammatical functions SUBJ(ect), OBJ(ect), OBJ$_\theta$ (restricted object) and OBL(ique) as follows:

(22)   SUBJ = $[-r, -o]$
     OBJ = $[-r, +o]$
     OBJ$_\theta$ = $[+r, +o]$
     OBL$_\theta$ = $[+r, -o]$

---

[6]See Chapter 2, section 2 below.

Each argument of each predicate comes to us classified into a thematic role type. The particular universal set of thematic role types and the hierarchy assumed is (exper. = experiencer):

agent < beneficiary < exper./goal < instrument < patient/theme < locative

(Of course this begs the question of how exactly to decide the appropriate classification, especially for difficult cases, which is the main question concerning us here.) These roles are mapped onto intrinsic classifications by the features $[+/-o]$ or $[+/-r]$ in accordance with certain typological generalizations, such as that 'patientlike roles may alternate between subject and object while other roles such as agent and e.g. locatives alternate between the nonobject functions.' (Bresnan and Zaenen 1990:50) Thus for example patients will be intrinsically classified as $[-r]$ (see (22)).

The predicate together with its thematic role classifications and intrinsic classifications is called an a(rgument)-structure. The idea is that 'the a-structures of words contain the minimal lexical information needed for the projection of semantic roles onto surface syntactic functions.' (Bresnan and Zaenen 1990:50) A monotonic theory maps these underspecified roles onto grammatical functions such as SUBJ and OBJ by filling in those features not provided by the intrinsic classification, much like the theory of feature underspecification in phonology.

Consider our earlier example again: suppose it is true cross-linguistically that Patients are intrinsically classified as $[-r]$ (i.e. they are subjects or objects but not 'restricted objects' or obliques). Recall that the a-structure includes both the thematic role classification and the intrinsic classification. If the mechanism for mapping from a-structures to grammatical functions (f-structures) is not sensitive to the thematic role classification (here, Patient) but only to the intrinsic classification (here, $[-r]$), then the question arises as to why thematic role classifications should be needed at all. But in fact some LMT analyses assume that this mapping is sensitive to thematic role classifications; an example is the rule of Theme Suppression in Bresnan and Moshi 1990:170.

Assuming for the sake of argument that such rules could be eliminated, then we might imagine a system that avoided thematic role classifications altogether. Instead, whatever semantic characterization which would otherwise be associated with the thematic role types would be associated directly with the intrinsic classification. Roughly speaking this is what Zaenen (1993) proposes. In particular, she associates Dowty's Proto-Agent and Proto-Patient with the features $[-o]$ and $[-r]$, respectively. In Zaenen's proposal the procedure in (21) is applied to an argument to derive the intrinsic classifications: a role with more Proto-Agent than

Proto-Patient properties is classified [–o] while a role with more Proto-Patient than Proto-Agent properties is classified [–r].

I believe the best way to look at such proposals as Dowty 1991, Bresnan and Kanerva 1989, and Zaenen 1993 is that they involve, first of all, a basic classification of arguments for the purpose of syntax: in Dowty's case this is expressed in the subject and object selection rules in (21), while for the two versions of LMT it is the Intrinsic Classification. There is not a one-to-one mapping between these syntactic classes and semantic classes. Instead there is a one-to-many mapping. Thus there is no semantic feature or set of features common to all (intrinsically) [–o] arguments or all [–r] arguments, but some procedure such as (21) is specified.

2.4 Lexical decomposition approaches

Lexical decomposition approaches are similar to thematic role theories, but they are sometimes claimed to make possible the sort of explicit semantics which thematic role theories lack. However, this apparent difference is illusory. This illusion is due to a confusion between logical formulae (such as formulae of intensional logic) and logical forms.

As a concrete demonstration of this point consider the study of Aktionsarten or lexical aspect. Aktionsarten categories are generally differentiated along the two dimensions of temporal criteria and agency. For example, the Dowty 1979 system has the following temporal categories: states, activities, single changes of state, and complex changes of state. Each of these is further split into agentive and non-agentive predicates. The fundamental temporal criterion is the notion of temporal change. Predicates involving change can only be true of intervals of time, not of single points of time (Dowty 1979, ch. 3). This is intuitively clear since temporal change minimally involves some individual undergoing a transition from lacking to having a given property and hence requires at least two points of time in order for a statement of such change to have a truth value.

This criterion of change separates states, which do not involve change, from the other three categories, which do. Activity predicates for Dowty denote indefinite change of state, while the remaining non-stative classes (single and complex change of state) denote definite changes. Activities and change of state predicates correspond to Vendler's (1967) activity and accomplishment categories, respectively. Examples of the former are the predicates *run* or *push a cart*, which lack definite criteria for completion; examples of the latter are *build a house* or *paint a chair*, which have such criteria (the existence of a house or painted chair).

Using the Montague grammar framework, Dowty (1979) made an explicit proposal for representing these classes. The basic idea is that the different aspectual properties of the various kinds of verbs can be explained by postulating a single homogeneous class of predicates— stative predicates— plus three or four sentential operators and connectives. (Dowty 1979:71)

The operators and connectives are treated as logical constants, with a standard model-theoretic interpretation for each.

Two important operators are CAUSE and BECOME. Accomplishments are defined in terms of the operator CAUSE, which takes two propositions as arguments. As its name suggests, this operator is meant to capture the notion of causation (for which Dowty develops an analysis in terms of relative accessibility of possible worlds). The BECOME operator takes a single state as its scope. As one would expect, its interpretation is fixed so that BECOME(p) is true at time t if $\neg p$ is true just prior to t and p is true just after t. This operator is introduced by accomplishment verbs, and the state p corresponds to the result state of the accomplishment.

As noted above, Dowty (1979) was not concerned with the issues of syntactic argument projection which will be central to this dissertation. But it is clear that a parallelism exists between his primitive operators and at least some of the thematic role types. For example, Dowty's translation of a transitive accomplishment verb like *open* is an expression of the form ϕ CAUSE y, where ϕ is an expression for a proposition containing a variable x and y is an expression of the form BECOME(p), where p is a state involving a variable y:

(23) $\lambda y \lambda x[\, x \, \text{DO} \, [[. \, . \, .x \, . \, . \, .] \, \text{CAUSE} \, [\text{BECOME}[\text{open}(y)]]]]$

The rules of syntactic/semantic combination ensure that x will correspond to the subject and y to the object of the sentence. So if we were interested in developing a thematic role system on the basis of Dowty's 1979 system, we could define two of our role types with respect to lexical translations of verbs which take the form (23). The names Agent and Theme for x and y respectively would not be unreasonable abbreviatory labels for such role types.

It should be noted, however, that to do so would in a sense be doing violence to the Montague system. The expressions of intensional logic are not meant to constitute a linguistic level of representation as is the Logical Form of GB and certain other linguistic theories. This is true even at the lexical level, since various aspects of the translation of a word can effectively be traded in for an appropriate meaning postulate. As Dowty (1979:199) notes

...it is not necessarily the form of a particular complex translation or meaning postulate that is literally significant, but the more subtle claim that word meanings of certain kinds are always constructable out of a certain fixed set of primitive semantic operations (here represented by the interpretations of operators such as CAUSE and BECOME) and stative properties.

In other words, the proposal does not require that there be a unique translation of each linguistic expression into intensional logic, but only that there be at least one translation.

In principle it is possible to adopt the mechanisms of Dowty's system and then proceed to define a linguistic level representing lexical decomposition. Two examples of research along those lines are the Role and Reference Grammar (RRG) developed by Foley and Van Valin (1984) and recent work by Manfred Bierwisch (1988).

Foley and Van Valin explicitly base their system on that of Dowty 1979. They develop a theory of what they call logical structures, very much along the lines laid out in hypothetical terms above. Thematic roles are defined according to the position a variable occupies in such a logical structure (Foley and Van Valin 1984:47ff.) For example, the sentence *The cat is on the mat* has the logical structure **be-at'**(the cat, the mat). A table of universal correspondences between positions in logical structure and thematic roles tells us that *the cat* is a Theme and *the mat* is a locative. A hierarchy of thematic roles then maps these onto the 'Macro-Roles' ACTOR and UNDERGOER, and these in turn are mapped onto the morphosyntax of the sentence.

For the present discussion we do not need to go into the details of the RRG systems of mapping from logical forms to thematic roles, and from thematic roles to morphosyntax. The important step is the mechanism which generates the logical forms in the first place. This mechanism crucially relies on taking expressions of intensional logic (IL) and reinterpreting them as expressions of logical form. For the purposes of doing Montague semantics it is not crucial that a sentence correspond to a unique IL expression, where this means uniqueness of form— as Dowty points out in the quote above. With regard to aspect Dowty's 1979 hypothesis was just that word meanings can be constructed out of states plus some combination of his operators. But for Foley and Van Valin the particular form of the logical expression is crucial, since otherwise there is nothing to prevent one from analyzing a sentence into a different logical structure and thus yielding a different thematic role classification.

An interesting wrinkle on the logical form approach to linking is due to Manfred Bierwisch (1988). As in the systems described above,

Bierwisch's semantic form (SF) contains operators from a finite universal list such as DO-CAUSE, BECOME, etc. Bierwisch hypothesizes that the tendency for mapping to grammatical functions to follow a 'thematic hierarchy' follows from a universal embeddedness principle which says that arguments are ordered according to the level of embeddedness in SF. Arguments corresponding to variables which are less embedded precede arguments corresponding to variables which are more embedded. This ordering determines the mapping to morphosyntax and to grammatical relations. For example, in a logical form like (23) above, the variable x would precede y, since y is more deeply embedded; because of the ordering on morphosyntactic features, x will be the grammatical subject (linked by agreement) and y the grammatical object (linked by adjacency). Thus with respect to linking this universal embeddedness principle serves the same function that a thematic hierarchy serves for thematic-role based theories.

Like Foley and Van Valin's, Bierwisch's approach relies on the assumption that each clause can be mapped to a unique SF, or at least that all SFs associated with a given clause have the same relative embedding of variables. But as we have seen, it appears that this assumption is not justified.

2.5 The problem of semantic primitives

At the beginning of section 2.2 we asked how roles are classified into thematic role types. More broadly, we must ask: what is the primitive semantic basis for our theory? How do we know a semantic primitive when we encounter one? What sort of criteria should we impose?

The strongest answer to the last question is that we should ask for some sort of *independent justification* for whatever semantic primitives we propose. A general weakness of thematic role types as well as lexical decomposition systems is that the primitive thematic roles or relations are not independently required by the grammar. Even semantic tests such as adverbial modification do not seem to point to a unified notion of Agent, due to the fragmentation problem Dowty (1986) pointed out (see section 2.2 above): some adverbs diagnose the presence of a volitional agent, some an initiating agent, and so on. Cover terms like 'Agent' and 'Theme' do not seem to be independently justified.

One answer to this problem which has been advanced is that thematic roles are *conceptual* primitives which are in principle independent of language and exist external to linguistic knowledge. According to one version of this idea thematic roles must meet a condition of 'epistemological priority' allowing them to form the basis for language acquisition. This possibility is put forth, albeit somewhat guardedly, in Chomsky 1981:10:

We may select a primitive basis of concepts in terms of which the others are definable, and an axiom system from which the theorems are derivable. ... The primitive basis must meet a condition of epistemological priority. That is, still assuming the idealization to instantaneous language acquisition, we want the primitives to be concepts that can plausibly be assumed to provide a preliminary, pre-linguistic analysis of a reasonable selection of presented data, that is, to provide the primary linguistic data that are mapped by the language faculty to a grammar; relaxing the idealization to permit transitional stages, similar considerations still hold. It would, for example, be reasonable to suppose that such concepts as 'precedes' or 'is voiced' enter into the primitive basis, and perhaps such notions as 'agent-of-action' if one believes, say, that the human conceptual system permits analysis of events in these terms independently of acquired language.

It strikes me as reasonable to impose some version of Chomsky's criterion of 'epistemological priority' on primitives of universal grammar (UG), including the semantic features in terms of which the argument selection generalizations are captured. Unfortunately it is difficult to apply this criterion in practice.

In a related vein, Jackendoff (1983) justifies semantic primitives by bringing information to bear from different cognitive domains, under the assumption of his Conceptual Structure Hypothesis (Jackendoff 1983:17):

There is a *single* level of mental representation, *conceptual structure,* at which linguistic, sensory, and motor information are compatible.

Concerning his *Cognitive Constraint*, which holds that this neutral level of conceptual structure is required, Jackendoff admits that it is 'difficult to see how to apply it usefully. Our notions of the information conveyed by nonlinguistic peripheral systems are if anything feebler than our undertanding of linguistic information.' (Jackendoff 1983:18) At this stage it seems that the study of cognition is not capable of providing independent evidence for or against particular grammatical analyses, and as a result there is very little support given for the specific conceptual structures which are claimed to be associated with sentences.[7] Like the epistemological

---

[7]Jackendoff does give some interesting data from 'pragmatic anaphora' (Hankamer and Sag 1976) in support of his vocabulary of conceptual categories:

(i)   a. Your coat is here [*pointing*] and your hat is there [*pointing*].
           PLACE

criterion, the Cognitive Constraint is an interesting hypothesis but difficult to confirm or falsify, or even to apply usefully on the assumption of its validity.[8]

3 Theoretical framework

For the purposes of representing subcategorization and phrase structure we will adopt the framework of Head-Driven Phrase Structure Grammar (Pollard and Sag 1987, 1992, 1994), with certain modifications described below.

In HPSG verbs and other predicators have a lexical feature SUBCAT which takes as its value a list of specifications for the various complements, where 'complement' is construed broadly to include subjects as well as objects and phrasal or clausal complements. The verb combines with these complements to form a complete or 'saturated' projection. The order of elements on the subcat list does not necessarily reflect surface linear order but rather the order of relative *obliqueness*, with more oblique elements appearing to the right of less oblique ones: PPs, VPs, and clausal complements are more oblique than NPs, and among the NPs the objects are more oblique than the subject. Thus in English all subcat lists can be embedded within the following regular expression:[9]

(24)   NP (NP) (NP) XP*   (where X≠N)

For example the subcat list for an intransitive verb contains one NP (a), while the subcat list for a transitive verb contains two NPs (b), and so on.

---

     b. You shuffle cards this way [*demonstrating*].
       MANNER

The idea is that pragmatic anaphora is understood at a cognitive level 'where visual and linguistic information are compatible.' (Jackendoff 1983:48)

[8]I am not denying the possibility that there may be important parallels between linguistic structure and other forms of cognition. It would be surprising if there were none.

[9]For simplicity I restrict myself to NP subjects, ignoring the possibility of analyzing some PPs (*In the room sat John*) and VPs (*To err is human*) as subjects.

(25) Some subcat lists.   <u>examples</u>

    a. died   < NP >   The lizard died.

    b. chased < NP, NP >   Felix chased Fido.

    c. tried   < NP, VP[*inf*] >   The lizard tried to get away.

    d. relied   < NP, PP[*on*] >   John relied on his cat.

    e. forced < NP, NP, VP[*inf*] > Felix forced the lizard to leave.

The universal Subcategorization Principle requires that heads combine with complements in such a way that the subcat value of the phrase (the 'mother node') is obtained by cancelling one member from the head daughter's subcat list for each complement actually appearing (i.e. phonologically) within the phrase. The Subcategorization Principle licenses the following structure for the combination of the verb *chased* with the complement NPs *Fido* and *Felix*:

(26)

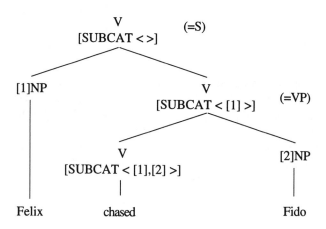

This is similar to cancellation of categories in categorial grammar, except that HPSG, unlike some categorial grammars, allows more than one item to be cancelled at a time.[10] For example, assuming a flat structure for

---

[10]Pollard and Sag (1987:71) state the Subcategorization Principle as the following constraint on headed structures:

ditransitive VPs, as we will below, the subcat list items for the two object NPs are both canceled at once, from the right-hand end of the subcat list:

(27)

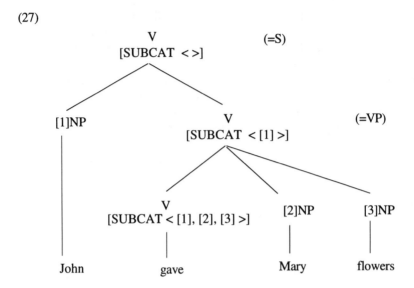

The linear order of sister complements such as *Mary* and *flowers* in (27) is determined by linear precedence (LP) rules. These LP rules are independent of the subcat list order in principle, although in practice LP rules may refer to the relative obliqueness (i.e. relative position on the subcat list), as in the LP rule stating that less oblique sister co-complements precede more oblique ones. This rule is proposed, with some revisions, in Sag 1985 and Pollard and Sag 1987.

$$[\text{DTRS}_{headed-structure}\ []] \Rightarrow$$

$$\begin{bmatrix} \text{SYN|LOC|SUBCAT} & [1] \\ \text{DTRS} & \begin{bmatrix} \text{HEAD} - \text{DTR|SYN|LOC|SUBCAT append}([1],[2]) \\ \text{COMP} - \text{DTRS} & [2] \end{bmatrix} \end{bmatrix}$$

This constraint says that a phrasal sign *A* must be such that the subcat list of *A*'s head daughter is the result of appending *A*'s subcat list to *A*'s complement daughters list in the order shown (where, e.g., append(<a,b>,<c,d>)=< a,b,c,d >).

(28)   COMPLEMENT$_1$ < COMPLEMENT$_2$
       where COMPLEMENT$_1$ is less oblique than COMPLEMENT$_2$

This rule is responsible for ordering the two sister NPs in (27) so that the more oblique object (*flowers*) precedes the less oblique one (*Mary*).

In tree diagrams like (26) and (27) the preterminal nodes represent signs while terminal nodes (*John, gave, Mary,* and *flowers* in (27)) merely serve to indicate the values for the phonology features of the associated preterminals, so there is no lexical insertion in the usual sense. The boxed numerals are tags representing token-identity as required by some linguistic constraint such as, in this instance, the Subcategorization Principle.

Immediate dominance (ID) schemata of HPSG are similar to standard X-bar schemata of GB theory (cp. Chomsky 1986):

(29)   a.   Specifier rule: $X'' \rightarrow Y''$, X'
       b.   Complement rule: $X' \rightarrow X$, Y''
       c.   *specifier* of X' =$_{df}$ $[Y'', X'']$
       d.   *complement* of X =$_{df}$ $[Y'', X']$
       e.   *head* of X^{n+1} =$_{df}$ $[X^n, X^{n+1}]$

The HPSG analogue of schema (29a) is a subtree in which a fully saturated (SUBCAT < >) category immediately dominates a mono-unsaturated category (a SUBCAT with exactly one element) and the complement saturating that one position.

(30)

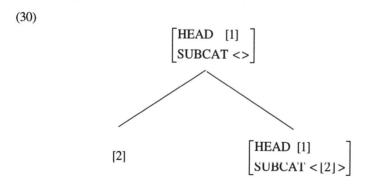

This schema subsumes the S $\rightarrow$ NP VP rule, for example. Corresponding to (29b) is an ID schema for a subtree in which a fully saturated category immediately dominates a polyunsaturated category (a SUBCAT list with more than one element) and complements saturating all but one element of this list.

(31)

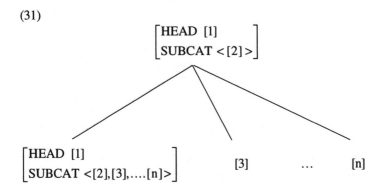

This ID schema subsumes VP expansion rules (VP → V NP), among others, since a VP has a mono-unsaturated subcat list ([SUBCAT < [2] > in (31)), the remaining item on its list corresponding to the subject or other specifier. Notice that all HEAD information such as major category is shared between the mother and its head daughter, as indicated by the tag [1]; the principle guaranteeing that this information is 'projected' from the head is the Head Feature Principle (see Pollard and Sag 1987:58).

In addition to its syntactic category (CAT), where the HEAD and SUBCAT features are found, the HPSG structure representing each constituent has a component called its semantic CONTENT, which contains linguistic information relevant to semantic interpretation. Thus each node label in the above trees would be more fully spelled out with a feature structure of the form in (32).

(32)

$$\begin{bmatrix} \text{CAT} & \begin{bmatrix} \text{HEAD} & [\ ] \\ \text{SUBCAT} & <...> \end{bmatrix} \\ \text{CONTENT} & [\ ] \end{bmatrix}$$

Following is the lexical entry for the verb *chases,* in the framework of Pollard and Sag (1994:29).

(33) *chases*

$$
\left[
\begin{array}{ll}
\text{CAT} & \left[\begin{array}{ll} \text{HEAD} & \textit{verb} \\ \text{SUBCAT} & < \text{NP}[\textit{nom}]_{[1][3rd,\ sing]}, \text{NP}[\textit{acc}]_{[2]} \end{array}\right] \\[4ex]
\text{CONTENT} & \left[\begin{array}{ll} \text{RELN} & \textit{chase} \\ \text{CHASER} & [1] \\ \text{QUARRY} & [2] \end{array}\right]
\end{array}
\right]
$$

This CONTENT value of this sign indicates that the verb *chases* encodes the chase relation (RELN), and that the CHASER and QUARRY roles are filled by the referential indices (or parameters) of the subject and object, respectively (see below for explanation of parameters).

For the first four chapters of this work, I will modify Pollard and Sag's system by positing that the set of argument slots, like the SUBCAT set, is ordered, as shown in (34). This innovation will make possible the sort of linking theory sketched in the introductory section above. Chapter 4 gives a reformulation of the theory which involves moving the ordering out of the CONTENT, among other changes.

(34) *chases*

$$
\left[
\begin{array}{ll}
\text{CAT} & \left[\begin{array}{ll} \text{HEAD} & \textit{verb} \\ \text{SUBCAT} & < \text{NP}[\textit{nom}]_{[1][3rd,\ sing]}, \text{NP}[\textit{acc}]_{[2]} > \end{array}\right] \\[3ex]
\text{CONTENT} & \left[\begin{array}{ll} \text{RELN} & \textit{chase} \\ \text{ROLES} & < [\text{CHASER}[1]], [\text{QUARRY}[2]] > \end{array}\right]
\end{array}
\right]
$$

The relation name (here the *chase* relation) is split off from this list of slots. In (34) 'NP$_i$' abbreviates an NP this structure:

(35)

$$
\left[
\begin{array}{ll}
\text{LOC} & \left[\begin{array}{ll} \text{CAT} & \left[\begin{array}{l} \text{HEAD } \textit{noun} \\ \text{SUBCAT} < > \end{array}\right] \\ \text{CONTENT}\,|\,\text{INDEX} & [i] \end{array}\right]
\end{array}
\right]
$$

The INDEX or *parameter* associated with an NP is roughly analogous to a logical variable. To understand the status of parameters and relations we need to review the basic features of Situation Semantics (Barwise and Perry 1983, Devlin 1991), the semantic theory adopted by Pollard and Sag (1987, 1994).

An important assumption of situation theory is the notion that relations (and properties, or one-place relations) are *basic*, in the sense that they are not defined in terms of anything else. Relations are not represented as sets, or sets of ordered pairs, etc., as they are in theories such as Montague grammar. The philosophical basis for this approach is a certain version of philosophical realism: a cognitive agent is said to possess a 'scheme of individuation' according to which it individuates (picks out, recognizes) certain individuals and relations in the world.

Each relation comes with a set of argument slots, to be filled with individuals or other objects. The basic unit of information, called a *state of affairs* or *soa*, is the information that some individuals or other entities do or do not stand in a given relation. Soas are notated with double angled brackets around a list of symbols representing, from left to right, the relation, the objects standing in the relation, and a polarity of value 1 (yes, they do stand in this relation) or 0 (no, they do not)). For example, assuming that 'liking' is a three-place relation between two individuals and a time, then the soa (36) represents the information that John liked Mary at the moment of 12:55:51 on August 2, 1991:

(36) « *LIKE*, liker:*John*, likee:*Mary*, time:*8/2/91:12:55:51*, polarity:*1*»

Next we need to consider the relation between this information and the world. Typically a piece of information does not concern the entire world taken as a whole, but rather a relatively small piece of the world (exceptions to this generalization are mathematical truths). Such pieces of the world are called *situations*. One novel aspect of situation semantics is that situations are treated as first class citizens of the ontology, alongside individuals, relations, and a few other items such as locations and times. A situation s is said to *support* a soa i (notated $s \models i$) if i is true by virtue of the internal structure of s. (A sort of maximal situation is the situation consisting of the entire world.)

We can think of a soa as giving rise to an issue: in the situation in question, do these individuals stand in this relation or not? While the individuation of the relation and of the individuals depends upon the agent's particular cognitive scheme, the resolution of this *issue* depends on the facts of the world. Either the (agent-individuated) objects do or do not stand in the (agent-individuated) relation in question, within the (agent-individuated) situation. Thus a particular supports relation $s \models i$ is fundamental in the sense that it is a fact about the world that this relation holds or does not hold.

To take a linguistic example, let us try to get at the content of the English sentence $\Phi = John\ kissed\ Mary$. Normally when someone utters this sentence they implicitly refer to a certain situation (called the *described situation*), one that includes at least John and Mary, and probably other relevant items. For example, in a conversation about a party the night before, the described situation would be the party or perhaps some subpart of it. Call this described situation s_1. If the utterer of Φ is telling the truth, then s_1 supports the information that John kissed Mary, as represented in (37).

(37) $s_1 \vDash$ « *KISS,* John, Mary, *t,* 1»

(The time t of the described situation precedes the time of utterance in this case, since the sentence Φ is in the past tense; we will ignore tense now for simplicity. Also for readability I have left out the labels of the slots such as 'kisser:', 'kissee:', 'time:' and 'polarity:'.) In order to get from this single utterance to the semantic content of the sentence Φ in general, we type-abstract over s_1, yielding the *situation type* S, the type of situation such that (37) holds.

(38)   S = [$s \mid s \vDash$ « *KISS,* John, Mary, *t, 1* »]

That is, S is just the type of situation which involves John kissing Mary. The situation type S roughly gets at the semantic content of Φ, but S actually contains more information than Φ, since we have ignored the problem of correctly associating the words *John* and *Mary* with the particular individuals John and Mary who occur in the soa in (37). Instead Φ might be paraphrased as 'someone named John kissed someone named Mary'. This indeterminacy is captured with the use of *parameters,* which are devices used to refer to arbitrary objects of a given type (such as the type 'individual'). We therefore replace the actual individuals John and Mary in this soa with parameters x and y for individuals.

(39)   S = [$s \mid s \vDash$ « *KISS, x, y, t, 1* »]

A function called an *anchor* assigns values to parameters ('anchors' them). Restrictions placed on this anchor can be spelled out explicitly; in the present instance x must be anchored to an individual named John and y must be anchored to an individual named Mary. These restriction are indicated in (40):

(40)   S = [s | s ⊨ « *KISS, x, y, t, 1* »]

x: « *NAMED, x*, John »

y: « *NAMED, y*, Mary »

(The temporal parameter t is similarly restricted, in this case to a time preceding the time of utterance, a matter we are ignoring here.)   In a particular utterance of Φ further restrictions on the anchoring of x and y might be supplied by the utterance context but the situation type S in (40) now accurately captures the descriptive content of the sentence Φ itself (Devlin 1991, section 5.2).

Parameters can also be used in the statements of general *constraints* of various kinds, which are linkages holding between situation types. An example from Devlin 1991, section 4.2 is the constraint that 'kissing means touching', the constraint in virtue of which one can infer that John touched Mary from the supposition that John kissed Mary. This is notated as follows:

(41)   [s | s ⊨ «*KISS, a, b, l, t, 1* »]

⇒{a,b,l,t}

[s | s ⊨ «*TOUCH, a, b, l, t, 1* »]

(where a and b are parameters for persons, and l and t are parameters for a location and a time respectively. The set {a,b,l,t} on the constraint arrow just indicates that this relation holds for any anchoring of $a,b,l,$ and t.) Barwise and Perry (1983:97) refer to such constraints, which stem directly from the agent's scheme of individuation, as *necessary* constraints. Notice that necessary constraints do the job performed in Montague semantics by meaning postulates (Dowty, Wall and Peters 1981:224ff), which are constraints on possible models.

Returning now to the HPSG formalism, let us consider how to represent these notions. The value of the CONTENT attribute for an NP has two features, one for the parameter and one for any restrictions placed by the content of the NP itself on the anchoring of the parameter. The lexical entry for the noun *book* would be the following:

(42) *book*

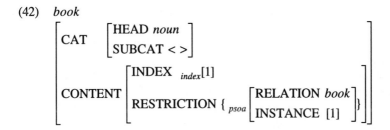

When the noun phrase *the book* appears as the complement of a verb, the index associated with the NP fills the corresponding argument role (see (33) and (34) above for examples of verbs). Through the value of the feature RESTRICTION, the anchoring of this referential index is restricted to objects with the property (i.e. one-place relation) of being a book.

Many of the details of HPSG and Situation Semantics are not crucial to understanding the first three chapters of this book. The key aspect of HPSG to be exploited is the functioning of the SUBCAT list, in which list items are cancelled from right to left as complements are combined with the head. However, Chapter 4, which presents some proposals for a more detailed formalization, assumes familiarity with the version of HPSG presented in Pollard and Sag 1994.

4 Overview

We propose that the problem of lexical semantics and complementation should be split into three types of constraint: (i) horizontal syntactic constraints on subcat structure; (ii) horizontal constraints on argument structure; and (iii) vertical constraints on the linking between subcat structure and argument structure:

(43) SUBCAT < ... ... > *principles of subcat structure*
              ⇑ ⇑
              linking *principles of linking*
              ⇓ ⇓
       ROLES < ... ... > *principles of argument structure*

The internal constraints on subcat structure will not be covered here; instead we focus on the other two components. In Chapter 2 we propose three semantic constraints on role ordering in argument structure. The first is based upon a single semantic primitive, the notion of 'notion' (Crimmins and Perry 1989, Crimmins 1989). With this single primitive we will essentially reconstruct the thematic role 'Agent' (perhaps 'cognitive agent' is a better term) in a very broad sense. The other two rules apply a primitive Part relation in two ways, first as the building block of a mereological theory of event structure (Hinrichs 1985, Krifka 1987), and secondly as a relation holding between coarguments of predicates like *contain* and *include*. Chapter 3 looks at the parochial classification of thematically restricted arguments via the theory of argument-sharing between verbs and prepositions. Chapter 4 gives a revised formulation of the theory in terms of a hierarchical inheritance lexicon of the sort proposed in Flickinger 1987.

2

Semantic Constraints on Argument Structure

1 Notions

1.1 Introduction

Crimmins and Perry (1989) present a theory of belief reports rooted in a straightforward logic of what they call *notions* (see also Crimmins 1989, Devlin 1991). It turns that out this logic of notions underlies the semantic constraints on the argument structure of a broad class of verbs, including psychological predicates (*want, believe, like, hate...*), perception verbs (*see, hear...*), and verbs of volitional action (*murder,...*). So let us begin by reviewing their theory.

Their proposal solves a class of doxastic puzzles exemplified by this story (Crimmins and Perry 1989:685):

In Mark Twain's *The Prince and The Pauper,* Tom Canty and Edward Tudor decide to change lives for a day, but fate intervenes, and the exchange goes on for a considerable period of time. The whole story turns on what people believe and don't believe about the two boys, and an intelligent reader, unexposed to recent philosophy of language and mind, could probably describe the key facts of the story with some confidence. Such a reader might explain why Miles Hendon, a penniless nobleman who encounters a boy dressed in rags, does not bow to the Prince, by noting:

(i) Miles Hendon did not believe that he was of royal blood.

And such a reader might ward off the implication that Miles was a fool or ignoramus by noting that Miles shared the dominant conception of Edward Tudor,

(ii) Miles Hendon believed that Edward Tudor was of royal blood.

The problem is that the reader would seem to be right on both counts (i) and (ii), despite the fact that *he* in (i) and *Edward Tudor* in (ii) refer to the same individual. The claim that both sentences are true appears to lead us to accept the doctrine of *opacity*, namely that the substitution of coreferring

31

names and demonstratives does not necessarily preserve truth.[1] The doctrine of opacity has certain undesirable consequences, which however need not concern us in detail here.[2] The solution Crimmins and Perry propose avoids opacity and seems to get at what is really going on in examples of this kind.

Crimmins and Perry approach this puzzle by focussing on the important fact that beliefs are *concrete cognitive structures,* mental entities distinct from the propositions which are the objects of beliefs. The object of a belief, sometimes called the belief's content, Intentional content, representative content, external content, or external significance, refers to the state of affairs in the 'external world' which holds iff the belief is correct. Two *different* beliefs can have the *same* proposition as content, which Crimmins and Perry argue is the case for the two beliefs reported in (i) and (ii) respectively.

To solve doxastic puzzles like the one above, the authors sketch out a theory of belief which starts by distinguishing the two simple facts that agents have beliefs and that those beliefs (normally) have contents (Crimmins and Perry 1989:689): the relation $B(a,b,t)$ holds of an agent, a belief and a time just in case b is a belief which belongs to the agent a at time t; and there is a partial function $Content(b,t)$ which, for a belief b and time t at which b exists, yields the content of b.

To implement such a theory one must look at the internal structure of beliefs. Beliefs are mental structures with *ideas* as constituents. Ideas are of at least two types: ideas of things, which are called *notions*, and ideas of properties and relations, which are called *property-ideas*.[3] The things and properties that ideas are *of* are called the *contents* of the ideas.

---

[1]Note that this applies specifically to names and demonstratives. 'Definite descriptions are another matter; it is not nearly as controversial that substituting a description for a coreferring name can influence the truth value of a report.' (Crimmins and Perry 1989:686, fn. 4)

[2]Opacity is incompatible with two other doctrines: (i) direct reference: the utterance of a simple sentence containing names or demonstratives normally expresses a 'singular proposition', i.e. a proposition constituted by the individuals referred to and not any descriptions of or conditions on them; (ii) semantic innocence: the utterances of embedded sentences in belief reports express just the propositions they would if not embedded, and these propositions are the contents of the ascribed beliefs.

[3]This terminology corresponds to that of Devlin 1991:166ff, as follows:

Crimmins and Perry	Devlin
idea	notion
notion	individual-notion
property-idea	relation-notion

The key to the puzzle above is just that Miles Hendon has two distinct *notions* with a single individual x (Edward Tudor) as content. These two notions were acquired in different ways. One of Miles' notions *of x* (i.e. with x as its content), call it n_{com} (*com* for common knowledge), was acquired in connection with other common knowledge of the royal family, and so Miles has a certain belief, with n_{com} as a constituent and with the propositional content 'x is of royal blood.' The other notion *of x*, call it n_{vis} (*vis* for visually acquired), was acquired when Miles saw a boy in rags. n_{vis} is also a notion of x because 'it was Edward with whom Miles was confronted when he formed this notion. Edward played the right part in the causal origin of the notion; that's what makes him its content.' (Crimmins and Perry 1989:5-6) So Miles lacks the belief, with this latter notion as a constituent, and with the propositional content 'x is of royal blood'. In sum, (i) and (ii) are both accurate belief reports, because they involve two *different* beliefs, one which Miles has and one which he lacks, but both with the same propositional content.[4]

The internal structure of a belief b is an ordered set consisting of a k-ary property idea and a sequence of k notions:

(44) $Structure(b) = \; <Idea^k, Notion_1, ... , Notion_k>$

The propositional content of a belief is the proposition that the objects its notions are *of* stand in the relation its property-idea is *of*. The content of the a belief with structure (44) at time t is:

---

[4]Keep in mind that ideas, like beliefs, are *concrete cognitive particulars*. They have nothing to do with Platonic ideals, for example. Devlin (1991) emphasizes their *physical* nature, since they are ultimately configurations in the brain.

> Notions are concrete structures realised in the brain. Exactly how they are realised is not relevant to our present discussion. They can arise as a result of perception (visual, aural, tactile, or whatever), or communication from another agent, or a combination of various means... (p. 166)

Ideas, like the beliefs they consitute, are not public; they belong to agents just as arms and teeth do. Similarly, two agents can have each his own belief but with the same proposition as content, in which case they believe the same thing. The locution 'A and B share this belief' is an imprecise way of saying that A's belief and B's belief, which are necessarily distinct, have the same propositional content.

(45) $Content(b,t) = < Of(Idea^k, t), Of(Notion_1, t), \ldots, Of(Notion_k, t) >$

Here *Of* is a (partial) function from ideas to their contents.[5]

For our purposes it will be useful to define the relation holding between an agent A, a notion n, and a time t just in case A has the notion n at time t. To have a notion n is just to have one or more Intentional mental state(s) in whose structure n is included.

(46) $Have(A,n,t) \leftrightarrow \exists m [M(A,m,t) \& Structure(m) = < \ldots n \ldots >]$

Where m is any Intentional (directed) mental state such as a belief, desire, or intention, and M is the corresponding relation of believing, desiring, or intending. An agent A is said to *Have* the notion n at time t just in case A has at least one such mental state with n as a constituent. Typically of course a single notion plays a role in many beliefs, desires, and so on.[6]

Next we define the *CONCEIVE* relation as holding between A, x, and t just in case A is an agent who has at least one notion of x at time t:

(47) $CONCEIVES(A,x,t) \leftrightarrow \exists n[Have(A,n,t) \& Of(n, t) = x]$

For example in the story above Miles Hendon *CONCEIVEs* of Edward Tudor; indeed he has two notions of Tudor.

---

[5]Some ideas have no content, so *Of* is a partial function.

[6]An essential aspect of this theory of notions is that an agent can have a single notion which enters into multiple 'mental structures' such as beliefs (Crimmins and Perry 1989, p. 692):

> Notions are the things in the mind that stand for things in the world. A notion is a part of each of a collection of beliefs (and, no doubt, of other mental structures, such as desires and intentions) that are *internally* about the same thing.

For example Miles could have numerous beliefs, desires, and intentions, all with n_{vis} (Miles' notion of the boy in rags) as a constituent part: a belief that the boy was being mistreated, a desire to help the boy, an intention to help the boy, etc. Within the confines of Miles' mind all the occurrences of n_{vis} are mutually consistent. They are all "internally about the same thing". This means that we have to be able to abstract away from particular beliefs and from particular *psychological modes* such as belief, desire, or intention and say that Miles simply "has" the notion n_{vis}.

To summarize, the key semantic primitive which forms the building block of this system is the notion that cognitive agents have 'notions'. Notions are related to real things and real relations via the *Of* function, a (partial) function from notions to their contents. From the point of view of linguistics, the point is that a semantics of belief reports which classifies them solely by propositional content is inadequate. To give the truth conditions for belief reports requires that one ascertain just which notions are involved in the beliefs being reported. This means that to the extent that our rules of argument selection stay within the ontology just described, we are not adding new semantic primitives but merely using semantic primitives which are independently known to be essential for the semantics of natural language.

1.2 The Notion-Rule

We begin with transitive sentences which report psychological states of various sorts. Under each sentence is an accompanying entailment, and a non-entailment:

(48)   a. John wants the cat.
            ⊨ John has a notion of the cat.
            ⊭ The cat has a notion of John.

        b. John likes Mary.
            ⊨ John has a notion of Mary.
            ⊭ Mary has a notion of John.

        c. John fears Mary.
            ⊨ John has a notion of Mary.
            ⊭ Mary has a notion of John.

        d. John is expecting Fred.
            ⊨ John has a notion of Fred.
            ⊭ Fred has a notion of John.

In order to *want*, *like*, *fear*, or *expect* some individual x, John must have a notion of x, since that notion plays a role in the structure of John's mental state of wanting, liking, fearing, or expecting: it is the 'object' (content) of his wanting, etc. But it is not necessary that x has a notion of John: for all we know the cat in (48a) could be unconscious. The generalization suggested by this entailment pattern is just that each sentence entails that the individual denoted by its *subject* NP has a notion of the individual denoted by its *object* NP, while the converse entailment does not go through. (The apparently exceptional 'experiencer-object' verbs like *frighten* and *please* are discussed in section 1.3 below.)

We now state a constraint on lexical signs to capture this generalization, using the *CONCEIVES* relation defined above as a relation holding between an agent *A*, an individual *x* and a time *t* just in case *A* has a notion of *x* at time *t*.

(49)   « *CONCEIVE, x, y, t* »

By convention we will let the left-hand slot (immediately to the right of the relation name) be for the Agent (filled here by the parameter *x*) and the let the slot to its right be for the entity which that Agent has a notion of. So (49) abbreviates (50):

(50)   « *CONCEIVE,* agent:*x*, entity.agent.has.a.notion.of:*y*, time:*t* »

Our constraint will work by forbidding certain lexical entries. It forbids any lexical entry whose content includes a relation and role list such that the relation involves the filler of the lower slot *CONCEIVE*-ing of the filler of the higher slot.

(51)   The Notion-Rule.

A lexical sign meeting this description is ill-formed:

$$* \begin{bmatrix} \text{REL} & R \\ \text{ROLES} & <...[\text{ROLE1}]...[\text{ROLE2}]...> \end{bmatrix},$$

if the following lexical entailment holds:
$\forall x, y \,\square[R \,(\text{ROLE1}:y, \text{ROLE2}:x) \rightarrow CONCEIVE(x,y)]$

Take for example the verb *like*. The following entailment holds for the **like** relation:

(52) $\forall x, y \,\square[\textbf{\textit{like}}(\text{LIKER}:x, \text{LIKEE}:y) \rightarrow CONCEIVE(x,y)]$

That is, *x* liking *y* necessarily involves *x* conceiving of *y*. Substituting the likee and liker roles for ROLE1 and ROLE2, the Notion-Rule tells us that the following is an ill-formed lexical entry:

(53)

$$* \quad \begin{bmatrix} \text{REL} & like \\ \text{ROLES} & < [\text{LIKEE}], [\text{LIKER}] > \end{bmatrix}$$

while this is a well-formed entry:

(54)

$$\begin{bmatrix} \text{REL} & like \\ \text{ROLES} & < [\text{LIKER}], [\text{LIKEE}] > \end{bmatrix}$$

This is the desired result. By the Isomorphy Condition, these unrestricted roles link up to complements without crossing lines.

(55)

$$\begin{bmatrix} \text{SUBCAT} & < NP_{[1]}, NP_{[2]} > \\ \text{ROLES} & < [\text{LIKER}[1]], [\text{LIKEE}[2]] > \end{bmatrix}$$

By the Subcategorization Principle the rightmost NP ($NP_{[2]}$) is added to the verb first, in this case forming a VP, then the subject $NP_{[1]}$ is added.

Notice that John can like Mary without knowing her name is Mary; he might just know her as the secretary in the ichthyology department with whom he chats regularly. In general we make no assumption here as to the nature of *other* beliefs or mental states in whose structure the notion in question might play a role. Similarly, the truth of (48a) does not require that John knows that the object of his desire is a cat, nor that he would use the word *cat* to describe it. Rather it requires only that John have a notion of whatever individual the content of the NP *the cat* in (48a) is restricting.

Next consider perception verbs:

(56)   John saw the orange cat.
       ⊨ John has a notion of the cat.
       ⊭ The cat has a notion of John.

Can John be said to have a *notion* of the orange cat in (56)? The answer is yes, that this is precisely the analysis of perception which has been found essential by Crimmins (1989:115ff) as well as Searle (1984) and others. Recall for example Miles Hendon's visually acquired notion of Edward Tudor. The only difference from the earlier cases is that now the psychological mode is the mode of *visual experience*. (56) says that John had a visual experience of the orange cat.[7]

A perception verb like *see* has rough a paraphrase in the verb *appear*, only the role for the seen-thing is filled by the subject: in any case the one to whom some x appears must have a notion of x. The Isomorphy Condition (9) together with the Notion-Rule predicts for the verb *appear* that *at least one of the complements is restricted*. This prediction is correct for English, as the preposition *to* marks the agent role:

(57) a.   The Muses appeared to me and urged me to write this dissertation.
      b.   *The Muses appeared me and urged me to write this dissertation.

Verbs like *appear* do not violate the Isomorphy Condition, which only guarantees isomorphy for unrestricted roles:

(58) *appear*
$$\left[\begin{array}{l} \text{SUBCAT:} < \text{NP}_{[1]}, \text{PP}[to]_{[2]}, > \\ \text{ROLES:} < [\text{EXPERIENCER}[2]]^{[+r]}, [\text{THEME } [1]] > \end{array}\right]$$

Being a restricted role, as indicated by the value $[+r]$, the experiencer's line of association with the subcat list can cross any other (see Chapter 3 for extensive discussion of restricted roles). But there are no transitive verbs meaning something like *appeared* that would make (57b) grammatical; such verbs would violate either Isomorphy or the Notion-Rule. Similar facts obtain in French subject-stimulus perception verbs, where the experiencer appears in the semantically restricted dative case rather than the accusative:

---

[7]Perception verbs differ from psych verbs in that the nature of the psychological mode (visual experience) automatically specifies the *causal origin* of the mental state. This means that they lack the sort of ambiguities observed above for psych verbs. Recall that Miles' two notions of Edward Tudor, n_{vis} and n_{com}, differed in their respective causal origin. But in the case of a visual experience the causal origin is just vision. So (i) and (ii) entail one another:

(i)   Miles saw him. (him = Edward Tudor in rags)
(ii)   Miles saw Edward Tudor.

In both (i) and (ii) the notion Miles has is just n_{vis}. Because the notions which arise through perception are automatically tied to their causal origin, the senses are sometimes said to be 'presentational' rather than representational (Searle 1984).

(59)   a.   La Mort est apparue à Jean dans ses rêves.
            the death has appeared to Jean in his/her-pl. dreams
            'Death appeared to Jean in his dreams.'

       b.   La Mort lui est apparue dans ses rêves.
            the death him/her.DAT aux appeared in his/her-pl. dreams
            'Death appeared to him/her in his/her dreams.'

       c.   *La Mort est apparue Jean dans ses rêves.
       d.   *La Mort l'est apparue dans ses rêves.
            the death him/her.ACC aux appeared in his dreams

Here I assume that the dative is restricted to a limited semantic class of roles including experiencers.

Verbs of volitional action also abide by the Notion-Rule. For example we can associate an entailment and a non-entailment with a verb like *murder* :

(60)   Oswald murdered Kennedy.
            ⊨ Osward had a notion of Kennedy.
            ⊭ Kennedy had a notion of Oswald.

The intuition is clear that a murderer must have a notion of his victim, bearing in mind once again that Oswald could murder Kennedy without knowing the name of his victim. But in any case he necessarily has some notion of his victim. The psychological mode in this case is the mode of *intention.* If Oswald murdered Kennedy, then there must be an individual x named Kennedy such that Oswald had an intention to kill x.[8]

Consider these further examples of volitional action:[9]

---

[8]Suppose now that Oswald, being deranged, had an intention to walk to the window and kill the first man he saw. That man happened to be Kennedy, so he murdered Kennedy. It still follows that Oswald's intention included a notion of (the man named) Kennedy. Oswald just didn't know that the person his notion was of was (named) Kennedy. His notion pointed to the victim in a rather odd way, but it still pointed. In particular, that notion's way of 'pointing' was such that Oswald knew very little *else* about his victim, beyond his being the first person Oswald saw through the window. After all, notions can be vague and they can point to things in round-about ways. If Oswald intends to kill the first man he sees, then Kennedy must actually *be* the first man Oswald sees in order for it to be true that Oswald murdered Kennedy (when he killed the first man he saw).

[9]Examples due to Bill Ladusaw. See Ladusaw and Dowty 1987.

(61)　a. Fido is chasing Felix.
　　　　$\models$ Fido has a notion of Felix
　　　　$\not\models$ Felix has a notion of Fido

　　　b. Felix is fleeing Fido.
　　　　$\models$ Felix has a notion of Fido
　　　　$\not\models$ Fido has a notion of Felix

Sentence pairs of the form *X chases Y* and *Y flees X* seem to describe very nearly the same situation, which means that a theory of argument selection must zero in on the crucial semantic distinction between them. Our theory appears to do just that. Chasers differ from flee-ees in that chasers must have a notion of their chasees, and flee-ers differ from chasees in that flee-ers must have a notion of their flee-ees. Thus a situation where Fido is unintentionally rolling down a hill (he is dead or asleep) and Felix is fleeing for his life for fear of being crushed does not make (a) true, but it does make (b) true.

Conversely, a situation where Felix is unintentionally rolling down a hill (he is dead or asleep) and Fido is chasing him does not make (b) true but it does make (a) true. In each case the subject-denoted participant is a volitional agent while the object-denoted participant is not. One can chase a falling leaf or flee a tidal wave, but, in as much as leaves and tidal waves are incapable of having notions, falling leaves cannot flee, even if they are being chased, and tidal waves cannot chase, even if they are being fled.

Let us take stock of what we have found so far. We have looked at three verb types:

(62)　a.　mental states: *want, like, fear, expect...*
　　　 b.　perception: *see, hear, touch, smell ...*
　　　 c.　volitional action: *murder, chase, flee ...*

Argument selection for all three verb types is covered by the Notion-Rule.

1.3 Psych verbs
　　　Some stimulus-subject psychological predicates like *frighten* may seem at first blush to violate the Notion-Rule, but I will argue that they are consistent with the rule. For verbs like *terrorize* the argument structure is correctly predicted by the Notion-Rule, since the subject-denoted participant must be volitional; while for verbs like *terrify* which are not obligatorily volitional, the Notion-Rule fails to apply (another rule applies instead; see section 2).

(63) a. CIA agents/?*Hailstorms terrorized the people.
      b. CIA agents/Hailstorms terrified the people.

Neither verb violates the Notion-Rule. There is sometimes confusion about these verbs stemming from a failure to distinguish properly between the *cause* and the *content* of a mental state. Eventive verbs of the *frighten* type describe the causation of a mental state, but not the Intentional content of the resultant state:

(64) The movie frightened John.

Example (64) tells us that the movie caused John to experience fright, but it does not tell us what, if anything, is the Intentional content of that fright— what, if anything, John became frightened *of* as a result. This usage is sometimes called the causative-inchoative (Dowty 1991). Verbs like *fear*, on the other hand, tell us the content but not the cause. Hence (64) clearly does not entail (65):

(65) John feared the movie.

Of course it sometimes happens in actual situations that the cause and the content roles of a fear are filled by one and the same entity, and in some cases it is reasonable to infer from a linguistic report of the causation of a mental state that the entity serving as the cause serves as the content as well. For example, if you say that *The dog frightened the baby*, it is reasonable to conclude from this that the dog caused the baby to become frightened *of the dog*. But inferences of this kind cannot trigger the Notion-Rule, which applies only at the lexical level. The Notion-Rule applies only if it is a general property of situations involving x frightening y that they necessarily involve y having a notion of x, which is not the case, as we just saw.

It is probably because the roles of cause and content are often played by the same entity that philosophers and linguists need to remind us periodically that they are in fact distinct roles, as in David Hume's conclusion that

We must, therefore, make a distinction betwixt the cause and the object of these passions, betwixt the idea which excites them, and that to which they direct their view, when excited. (Hume 1968/1888:278).

In linguistics discussions similar observations have been made by Croft 1991, Grimshaw 1990, Pesetsky 1987, among others. The Notion-Rule allows us to zero in on the crucial distinction between the two halves of 'flip verb' pairs like *please/like* or *frighten/fear*. Contrasts like (66) show that the verb *please* does not violate the Notion-Rule, since x pleasing y does not necessarily involve y having a notion of x:

(66) a. As manager of Macy's department store, John has managed to please thousands of customers over the years. Most of them do not know John exists.
   b. Thousands of customers like John. #Most of them do not know John exists.
   c. Melvin hid behind a tree and made eery sounds, which fooled the tourists into thinking the house was haunted. In this way Melvin frightened the tourists.
   d. Melvin hid behind a tree and made eery sounds, which fooled the tourists into thinking the house was haunted. #In this way, the tourists feared Melvin.

Likewise, one can imagine situations making (67a) true in which the cat is not aware that there is anyone or anything at the other end of the string; and situations making (67b) true in which the children are unaware that anyone is in the business of amusing them.

(67) a. John amused the cat in the box by dangling a string through a hole.
   b. The Disney cartoonists have amused thousands of children over the years by creating a vivid cartoon world which the children mistook for reality.

Some further examples follow. Each of the words in this list could be substituted in one or more of the example sentences.

(68)   *cheer up, comfort, tantalize, terrorize, unsettle, shake up, harrass, pester, tease, delight, intrigue, fascinate, beguile, gall, confuse, puzzle, perplex, soothe...*

    a.   John thinks he can *cheer up* random strangers by leaving money on the sidewalk for them to find.
        ⊭ random strangers have a notion of John

    b.   The ghost *annoyed* the tenants by playing tricks on them.
        ⊭ the tenants have a notion of the ghost

    c.   Some kids switched the traffic signs around to *confuse* the drivers.
        ⊭ the drivers have a notion of the kids

    d.   The food was secretly laced with a mild sedative. This drug *calmed* the patients.
        ⊭ the patients have a notion of this drug

These examples are designed to make it possible for the experiencer to avoid awareness of the cause of his or her mental state. As a consequence some of the scenarios are a bit exotic. But the point is to diagnose the basic meaning of these words by teasing apart the cause from the content of the mental state. Some further stimulus subject verbs follow. I believe that the reader will find that scenarios on the pattern of those above can be constructed for all or nearly all of these verbs:

(69)   Some stimulus-subject verbs consistent with the Notion-Rule.
comfort, cheer (up), tantalize, startle, terrorize, indoctrinate, teach, instruct, deprogram, cow, shame, unsettle, shake up, discombobulate, harrass, pester, tease, please, amuse, tickle, delight, thrill, move, stir, arouse, excite, freak out, turn on, entrance, bewitch, bore, surprise, amaze, astound, astonish, awe, wow, confuse, puzzle, perplex, mystify, baffle, bewilder, boggle, stupefy, shock, dismay, appal, horrify, terrify, annoy, bother, irk, bug, vex, pique, nettle, irritate, provoke, gall, aggravate, grate on, piss off, anger, interest, rile, incense, infuriate, outrage, miff, frustrate, embarrass, disgust, gross out, worry, trouble, distress, upset, disturb, frighten, scare, alarm, grieve, hurt, pain, torment, soothe, calm, dumbfound, flabbergast, satisfy, charm, engage, captivate, exasperate, revolt, humiliate...

Of the above verbs, all are either obligatorily volitional and therefore covered by the Notion-Rule (*harrass, indoctrinate, terrorize*)[10]; or optionally volitional and therefore not covered by the Notion-Rule, but not counter-examples either since neither argument is entailed to have a notion of the other (*please, amuse, arouse*).

At the same time, there are a few verbs which appear to be genuine counter-examples to the Notion-Rule:

(70)   Stimulus-subject verbs violating the Notion-Rule.
       concern, preoccupy.

The list in (70) contains all the stimulus-subject verbs violating the Notion-Rule which I could think of. For x to concern or preoccupy y it seems that y must have some notion of x, as shown by the contradictory nature of (71a) and (b); and neither verb can be used volitionally (71c).

(71)   a.   #Toxic waste concerns the Senator deeply— he just happens to be unaware of its existence.
       b.   #The most recent massacre of defenseless civilians by the U.S. military was so brutal that it preoccupies even those who do not know that it occurred.
       c.   *John is trying hard to concern/preoccupy Mary, but she couldn't care less about him.

In contrast to the many verbs which are consistent with the Notion-Rule, these counter-examples are strikingly few in number, and this class of exceptional verbs shows no signs of growing.[11] (See Chapter 4 below for a treatment of exceptional verbs.)

A number of linguists (Croft 1991, Pesetsky 1987) have noted that the verbs of the *frighten* class are, as Grimshaw (1990:23) writes, 'causative and not stative', in contrast with the *fear* type, which are stative according to

---

[10]An often repeated example which I have not listed in (69) or (70) is the verb *strike*, as in *John's request strikes Mary as strange.* I assume *strike* is a raising verb, i.e. that *John's request* is the raised subject of *as strange,* and is not a coargument of *Mary.*

[11]Interestingly, the linking for these two counter-examples is a common source of difficulty for second language learners of English, who occasionally make mistakes such as 'we concern syntax in this class' or 'she preoccupies memories of Japan', thus bringing these verbs into line with the demands of the Notion-Rule (this was pointed out to me by Peter Sells).

the Vendler (1967) classification. Grimshaw (1990:23) argues that 'considering verbs of the *frighten* class to be causative... provides immediate insight into their argument realization: the cause arguments of causative predicates are always subjects.' According to Grimshaw's proposal argument selection is determined by aspectual structure on a separate 'tier' from thematic structure (see also Tenny 1987 for a proposal to make aspect the sole interface between lexical semantics and syntax). Thematic structure is determined by the more or less standard thematic hierarchy shown in (72a) (Grimshaw places theme lower than locative while some authors place it higher); while the hierarchy determining aspectual structure is shown in (72b):

(72) a. agent < experiencer < goal/source/location < theme
      b. cause < other

However, her analysis leaves the *fear* type verbs unexplained, as she admits: 'The case of psychological state verbs like *fear* is considerably more delicate. The desired result will follow if their Experiencer qualifies as the aspectually most prominent argument... However, it must be admitted that in this case there is no independent evidence that the aspectual analysis will give this result so for the present purposes we must simply stipulate it.' (Grimshaw 1990:27-28) Neither tier correctly predicts the argument selection for both the *fear* and *frighten* types.[12]

The present proposal accounts for the *fear* type and for the volitional verbs of the *frighten* type, and the other verbs of the *frighten* type are not

---

[12]Grimshaw (1990:15) cites the following type of constrast as evidence for her two-tiered approach:

(i)   a. a god-fearing man
      b. *a man-fearing god ('a god whom men fear')
(ii) a. *a child-frightening storm
      b. *a storm-frightening child ('a child whom storms frighten')

In general the 'highest' argument is the externalized one, i.e. the one which is not incorporated into the compound (e.g. *man* in (ia)), which explains why (ib) and (iib) are bad. The question is why (iia) is bad. Grimshaw (1990:25) proposes that '[(iia)] is impossible because it requires the Theme to be theta-marked in a wider domain than the Experiencer, and [(iib)] is impossible because it requires the non-Cause to be theta-marked in a wider domain than the Cause.' That is, each violates the hierarchy on some tier. However, some compounds of the type in (iia) are acceptable, e.g.: *a crowd-pleasing politician*; *a bird-frightening device*.

problematical, they just have not yet been covered (non-volitional causation will be taken up in the section 2 below). The key feature of the present account is that it does not involve classifying one argument as an 'experiencer' in isolation from the coargument participants, but instead looks at the relation between two coarguments to see whether one participant necessarily has a notion of the other; this picks out the subject of *fear* but not the object of *frighten*.

1.4 Contractual verbs

Some contractual verbs (*hire, marry*) normally denote events involving two volitional agents, each with a notion of the other. This would contradict the Notion-Rule as stated, were it not that this appears to be a contingent fact about typical hiring, marrying, etc., and not intrinsic to situations of this kind. Slaves can be hired without knowing of their hirers (73a). It is somewhat less plausible that the hirer would not be aware of his hires, although if an employment agency hired workers on a boss's behalf then perhaps the boss could be said to have hired on some people without realizing it; in any event this latter case would not counterexemplify the Notion-Rule since it is the subject pariticipant who has a notion of the object and not vice versa. Marrying does not necessarily require consent of either party, as in arranged marriages of children (74).

(73)   a.   The plantation boss hired some slaves from their owners (without the slaves knowing of the plantation's existence).
       b.   The plantation boss hired some slaves (#without knowing of the slaves' existence).

(74)   a.   The Duke married the two-year old princess.
       b.   (?)The two-year old princess married the Duke.

If any strong cases of 'mutual conceiving' can be found, then the solution would be to amend the Notion-Rule so that it allows symmetrical conceiving between subject and object but disallows one-way conceiving of the subject by the object:

(75)   The Notion-Rule (revised).

A lexical sign meeting this description is ill-formed:

$$* \begin{bmatrix} \text{REL} & R \\ \text{ROLES} & <...[\text{ROLE1}]...[\text{ROLE2}]...> \end{bmatrix},$$

if the following holds:
$$\forall x,y \,\square\, [R \,(\text{ROLE1}:y, \text{ROLE2}:x) \rightarrow CONCEIVE(x,y)] \wedge$$
$$\neg \forall x,y \square [R \,(\text{ROLE1}:x, \text{ROLE2}:y) \rightarrow CONCEIVE(x,y)]$$

However, in the absence of clear examples of such cases we can continue to keep the Notion-Rule in its earlier form in (51).

2 Cause and effect

2.1 The Nuclear Role Rule

Many verbs remain which do not involve notions and so are not covered by the Notion-Rule, but which also exhibit semantic regularities in argument selection. Among them are verbs describing causal events which are never volitional, such as the following.

(76)   a.   The virus infected the organism.
      b.   The organism metabolized the sugar.
      c.   The acid dissolved the metal.
      d.   The sponge absorbed the water.

Generally speaking one cannot willingly metabolize, dissolve or absorb something, so notions play no role here. In the case of infecting, one can willingly infect someone with a disease but in any case it is not necessary, so the Notion-Rule will not apply. Indeed there are many verbs expressing actions which may be volitional but need not be:

(77)   a.   George/The fire killed seven people.
         (cp. #The fire murdered seven people.)
      b.   George unintentionally killed a cockroach (when he stepped on it).
      c.   John/The sun melted the ice cubes.

These verbs do not qualify for the Notion-Rule since it does not necessarily follow from x killing or melting y that x has a notion of y.

Verbs of this kind may be analyzed either in terms of the 'cause' or the 'effect' of the denoted action. According to the *causal* view (Croft 1991, Grimshaw 1990, inter alia) some participant is identified as the 'cause' of the action, and this participant is the subject argument: the sponge (not the water) causes the water to be absorbed; the acid (not the metal) causes the dissolution of the metal; and so on. Alternatively one might identify a participant as the one more *affected* by the action, and this participant is the object argument (Tenny 1987): the water (not the sponge) changes location as a consequence of its absorption; the metal (not the acid) ceases to exist as a consequence of its dissolution; and so on. And of course one might contend that both cause and effect are relevant. I will argue that the second view is the correct one: it is the *effect* that is relevant.

Taking (76c) for example, note that there is a clear asymmetry between the acid and the metal with respect to the effect of the event of dissolving. Roughly speaking the metal is more strongly 'affected' by the event; if the dissolution is total then the event ends when the metal ceases to exist as pointed out by Tenny (1987). More precisely, while both participants are affected by the action, the metal but not the acid is affected in a manner which is intrinsically tied to the individuation and temporal structure of the event itself: the dissolving-event is half over when the metal is half gone; the event is complete when the metal is completely gone. While the acid also undergoes a chemical change when it dissolves something, this change is not wedded to the temporal progression of the event.

In the terminology of Dowty 1991 the role of the thing which dissolves is an *incremental theme* role, since it changes state (goes out of existence, in this instance) incrementally, in lockstep with the progression of the event. He gives the example of the verb *mow,* the object argument (the mowee) of which has an incremental theme role:

For example, take the telic event described by *mow the lawn.* If I tell my son to mow the lawn (right now), and then look at the lawn an hour later, I will be able to conclude something about the 'aspect' of the event of his mowing the lawn from the state of the lawn, viz., that the event is not yet begun, or is partly done but not finished, or is completed, according to whether the grass on the lawn is all tall, partly short, or all short. By contrast, I will not necessarily be able to inspect the state of my son and conclude anything at all about the completion of his mowing the lawn. In this event, my son is the Agent and the lawn is the Theme, in fact the Incremental Theme. (Dowty 1991:567)

Krifka 1987 and Hinrichs 1985 give mathematically precise treatments of incremental themes and related thematic roles by applying Link's (1983) lattice-theoretic analysis of quantity to both objects and events, and then defining systematic relations between them. Simplifying Krifka's (1987) analysis somewhat, the realm of physical objects, including quantities of matter, is characterized by a predicate whose extension has the algebraic structure of a join semi-lattice, where the primitive PART relation relates any object (or quantity of matter) to its upper bound(s).

Take for example the wine in a glass; call this quantity of wine x_1. Any quantity of wine x_n one might pour out of the glass is a PART of x_1; x_n could in turn have a further subpart, and so on. Now take an event e_1 of drinking the wine in the glass; various wine-drinking events can be recognized as PART of e_1; these subevents of drinking wine could in turn have a further subparts, and so on. Thus the 'part structure' of the quantity of wine can be modelled as a lattice of objects, and the part structure of the event can be modelled as a lattice of events. Now for certain participants in an event, specific algebraic relations hold between the two lattices. If we let thematic roles be relations between objects and events, then these algebraic relations can be used to model thematic role types. In Krifka's terms a thematic role R is *gradual* if whenever $R(e,x)$ holds for an event e and object (or quantity of matter) x, there exists an e' which is part of e and an x' which is part of x such that $R(e',x')$. For example, the drinkee(e,x) role of *drink* is gradual: if drinkee(e,x) holds of a drinking event e and quantity x of liquid (i.e. e is an event in which x gets imbibed), then there is an event e' and a quantity of liquid x' such that drinkee(e',x') also holds, where e' isa sub-event of e and x' is a part of x.

Dowty (1991) suggested that incremental themehood was one contributing property of the Patient Proto-Role, as part of the proto-role system discussed in Chapter 1, section 2.3 above. In other words incremental themes tend to be objects of transitives or subjects of intransitives, but not subjects of transitives. For us this means that incremental themes lie at the righthand (low) end of the argument structure, that is, that non-incremental themes lie to the left of incremental themes.

Predicates like the following suggest that the object lattice should be extended to encode not only quantification in the strict sense but also other scalar properties like blackness (in 78a) or solidity (in 78b):

(78)   a.   The sun blackened the raisins.
        b.   The sun baked the bricks.
        c.   John grew old.
        d.   The light dimmed.

When the event in (78a) is half over we would not normally find that half the raisins are black but rather that all of the raisins are only somewhat black; similarly, in (78b) one would not normally find half the quantity of bricks baked first, then the other half; rather the bricks as a whole would become half-baked first. Dowty (1991) refers to these roles as *holistic themes*.

Like the incremental themes, holistic themes lie at the righthand (low) end of the argument structure. For still other predicates such as *kill*, the change of state of the victim (from alive to dead) is not gradual but sudden; but once again this change of state is inherently tied to the progression of the killing event, which is over when the victim dies.

All such roles for which a change of state in the participant filling them lends the denoted event its temporal constitution will be called *nuclear* roles, reflecting the fact that they are part of the aspectual 'nucleus' of the event. We state our argument selection rule as a constraint against lexical entries in which a lower role is non-nuclear while a higher role is nuclear:

(79)   The Nuclear Role Rule.

A lexical sign meeting this description is ill-formed:

$$* \begin{bmatrix} \text{RELN} & R \\ \text{ROLES} & <...[\text{ROLE1}]...[\text{ROLE2}]...> \end{bmatrix} ,$$

where ROLE1 is [+nuclear] and ROLE2 is [−nuclear].

This accounts for the examples we have seen. For example (80a) is a well-formed argument structure for *dissolve,* but (80b) is ruled out by the Nuclear Role Rule.

(80)   a.   *dissolve* < [AGENT, −nuclear] , [THEME, +nuclear] >
       b.   **dissolve* < [THEME, +nuclear] , [AGENT, −nuclear] >
            (ruled out by the Nuclear Role Rule)

This correctly predicts that the dissolved-thing role (the 'theme') is the object and not the subject of (76c).

There is linguistic evidence from English for the feature [±nuclear] from the interpretation of the verbal prefix *re-* (Wechsler 1989). Consider the entailments and presuppositions of the following examples.

(81) a. John reopened the door.
            entails: John opened the door.
            presupposes: *The door was previously open.*
      b. Mary repainted the wall.
            entails: Mary painted the wall.
            presupposes: *The wall was previously painted.*

In general if *re-S* is a sentence like *S* but with *re-* affixed to the verb, then *re-S* entails *S* and presupposes that a situation resembling the event denoted by *S* (or a subpart of that event) previously obtained. In what ways must the presupposed earlier situation resemble the denoted one? Specifically, which participants must be common to both? It turns out that all the participants with [+nuclear] roles must be common to both. In (81a) the event of opening a door is over exactly when the door becomes open; and in (81b) the wall becomes incrementally more painted as the wall-painting event progresses. But (81a) does not presuppose that it was necessarily *John* who previously opened the door, nor does (81b) presuppose that it was necessarily *Mary* who previously painted the wall.

      If we say that *re-* 'takes scope over' those arguments which must be part of the presupposed earlier situation (cp. Carlson and Roeper 1980, Roeper 1981), then the generalization can be stated as (82).

(82) *re-* takes scope over all [+nuclear] arguments.

The prefix *re-* also fails to take scope over [–nuclear] arguments such as instrumentals:

(83) Mary repainted the wall with a brush.

This does not presuppose that the earlier painting involved a brush; again this exemplifies (82): the instrumental argument is [–nuclear] since nothing about the state of the brush necessarily changes in lockstep with the event.

      The examples above are also consistent with an analysis of the semantics of *re-* according to which 'its meaning is that the result-state of an accomplishment is true for a second time, but not necessarily that the bringing about of this state occurs for a second time.' (Dowty 1979:256) In (84a) the satellite has been located within the earth's atmosphere on an earlier occasion (being in x is the result state of entering x), but it need not have entered before; and (84b) can be true even if no one has arranged the boulders before. It requires only that the boulders were once before in an 'arrangement'.[13]

(84) a. The satellite reentered the earth's atmosphere at 3:47.
     b. John rearranged the boulders on the hillside.

From this account of the meaning of *re-* it follows that only those participants which are part of the result state should be in the scope of *re-*.

However, there are other *re-* verbs which apparently lack result states.[14]

(85) a. John reread *Ulysses* in one day.
     b. The instructor wasn't looking, so John had to reswim the last lap.
     c. John reran the last lap of the race for the TV cameras.
     d. The caravan recrossed the desert.

In (85b) and (c), for example, John's position is the same before as after swimming or running the lap. Of course the events described by these sentences will have consequences: if John read *Ulysses* in a day, his eyes were tired by the end of the day, and so on. But they lack a result state in the sense of a specific state built into the predicate which serves as a criterion for the action to be perfected.

We will call predicates such as those in (85) 'path accomplishments' since they involve movement along a path, either in space (*rerun, reswim, recross*) or along some more abstract dimension such as the text of a book (*reread*). With path accomplishments it is sometimes the case (not always; see presently) that both participants are [+nuclear], since it is the *relative* position of the two which changes incrementally as the event progresses. For example in (86a) it is the physical extent of the 'path' (the desert) which defines the length of the event while in (86b) it is the physical extent of the 'theme' (the train):

---

[13](84a) and (b) are both from Dowty 1979. He attributes the latter to James McCawley.

[14]Dowty (1979:186-187) noted that accomplishments like *read a book* pose a problem for an analysis like his which ties accomplishment-hood to the bringing about of a result state. The sentences in (85) pass the tests for accomplishments, but *re-* does not seem to signify that a state has been restored.

(86) a.   John crossed the desert in one hour.
  b.   The train crossed the border in ten minutes.

Since it is the *relative* position of the two participants which changes incrementally, both theme and path are criterial for the event's completion, so both are nuclear arguments.[15]

With the path accomplishments the set of roles which are [+nuclear] can depend on subtle shifts of interpretation. Interestingly, it turns out that as contextual factors force shifting interpretations of a sentence, the scope of *re-* shifts appropriately, as predicted by (82).

For example, on the most prominent reading of

(87)   John reswam the English Channel.

both John and the English Channel are within the scope of *re-*, as predicted by (82), since both arguments are nuclear. But there are also various marginal result state readings, where a swimmer's successful crossing crucially 'affects' the path. Suppose the swimmer's purpose is to inspect the floor of some channel floor for sunken treasure, a task which transforms an uninspected channel into an inspected one. Since the channel and not the swimmer is the sole affected participant, the swimmer argument falls outside the scope of *re-* , as in the following:

(88)   John swam the channel yesterday and found nothing; but I don't believe he looked carefully enough. So I'm going to reswim it today.

---

[15] A variation of this phenomenon occurs with ditransitive verbs like *(re)send,* as in *John re-sent Mary the book.* Strictly speaking the 'intended recipient' role filled by Mary is not nuclear, since the result state does not include Mary. That is, the sentence entials that Mary was the intended recipient of the book, but does not entail that Mary actually received the book. (This is my intuition, as least. Apparently there may be some variation among English speakers on this point.) Nevertheless, Mary is within the presuppositional scope of re-, as shown by the infelicity of the folowing: *John sent Sue the book, but Sue returned it. #So John re-sent Mary the book.* The reasons for this are not clear, but apparently for the purpose of predicting the scope of re-, the intended recipient effectively counts as if it were an actual recipient. See Chapter 3, section 4, for further discussion.

Indeed, in the last sentence of (88) the swimmer argument lies outside the scope of *re-*. For speakers who find such scenarios plausible, in this context transitive swim has only one nuclear argument.[16]

Reading resembles swimming in that the text being read acts as a path along which the reader moves, while the text itself is not affected by the reading process. Consider whether (89a) presupposes (b) or the stronger (b'):

(89) a. John reread the poem.
      b. 'Someone had previously read the poem.'
      b'. 'John had previously read the poem.'

(89a) clearly presupposes at least (89b), as predicted by (82), since the poem is an incremental theme. But was John necessarily the reader in the presupposed earlier reading event? If we assume (i) that John read the poem silently, and (ii) that he read passively, and not for the purpose of affecting the poem (he was not, e.g., proofreading or editing it), then (89a) does indeed presuppose (b'). However, if we drop one of those assumptions, then (89a) no longer presupposes (b'), but only the weaker (89b).

As an example of dropping the first assumption, suppose that (89a) describes an event at a poetry recital. The speaker could then felicitously say that Mary read the poem (aloud), and then John reread it, even if John never read it before. This has only the weaker presupposition (89b).

As an example of dropping the second assumption, suppose Mary and John are editors of a poetry journal who are proofreading the poem. Then one could say that Mary read the poem, and then, to be on the safe side, John reread it. Again, this contradicts the presupposition in (b') and has only the weaker presupposition that someone read the poem before. The interpretation of (89a) with the weaker presupposition (b) is a result state accomplishment, where completion depends on the attainment of a result state. But this result state includes only the proofread poem, which is affected by the action.

Now suppose John serves on an evaluation committee and read a report in order to evaluate its merits. Another committee member had

---

[16]Some speakers can get a historical result state reading, where swimming the Channel 'affects' it in some abstract sense by giving it the status of a conquered goal. In a discussion of swimmers throughout history who have managed to cross the English Channel, a speaker says

(i)   After Smith's famous crossing in 1930, the Channel remained unconquered for over 50 years. Finally, in 1986, a swimmer named Jones reswam the Channel.

already read the report, but the assiduous John felt obliged *to reread it*. Here John's act of reading amounts to extracting (and processing) information from the report. The task of extracting and processing this information is delimited solely by the report itself, so the agent becomes non-nuclear.

(90a) allows a distinct 'historical' result state interpretation (90b') in addition to its normal result state interpretation (90b):

(90) a. On Sept. 17 Dr. Jones reentered the crypt of the pharoah.
      b. 'Dr. Jones was inside the crypt prior to Sept. 17.'
      b'. 'Someone or something entered the crypt prior to Sept. 17.'

Normally the result state of *X entered Y* is 'X is located inside Y', so that *X reentered Y* presupposes that 'X was previously located inside Y'. On the normal reading of (90a), which presupposes (90b), Dr. Jones did not necessarily ever enter the crypt before. He may have been born inside the crypt, and never reentered until September 17. But some speakers also get a special 'historical' reading, which presupposes (90b'): Dr. Jones need never have been inside the crypt prior to September 17, the relevant background assumption being perhaps that Dr. Jones was the first to violate the sacred crypt in many years.

To summarize, in every case *re-* takes scope over the [+nuclear] argument(s), that is, the participant(s) in terms of which the denoted event is temporally ('aspectually') constituted. With theme-path verbs, there is a certain plasticity of interpretation: either the progression of the event is determined by the relative position of theme and path; or the progression of the event is determined by some effect upon the path participant. In the former interpretation both participants are [+nuclear] and both lie within the scope of *re-*; in the latter interpretation only the path participant is [+nuclear] and only it lies within the scope of re-.

In every case the argument selection is consistent with the Nuclear Role Rule (79). We never find verbs for which the subject argument is [+nuclear] (and in the scope of re-) while the object argument is [–nuclear]. For example, while *smoke* in (91) has an incremental theme role (the event is half over when half of the smoke has entered), (91b) shows that the room is filling a [+nuclear] role as well: there is no interpretation where smoke was previously in a *different* room, but not in room 101.

(91) a. Smoke entered room 101.
      b. Smoke reentered room 101.
          presupposes: Smoke was previously in *room 101*.

So in this case we have an interepretation of enter where both theme (smoke) and path (room 101) are [+nuclear]; this is consistent with the observation that it is the relative location of the smoke and room which is relevant.

2.2 Comparison with causal analyses of argument selection

Notice that in the above discussion we have not mentioned causation or attempted to identify a participant as the 'cause' of the event. This account has the advantage of avoiding the problem of attempting to define 'cause' as a relation between *objects* (individuals) and events.[17] For example in (92) it is difficult to say with precision why there is any asymmetry between the acid and the metal with regard to the cause of the event.

(92)   The acid dissolved the metal.

Instead the cause of this dissolving event is a situation involving both acid and metal, and perhaps other factors such as temperature as well: when the acid and the metal are in contact under the appropriate conditions then dissolving will occur. Dowty (1979:91-99) argued against the generative semantics analysis of causation as a relation between an individual and a proposition. Instead he defines CAUSE as a relation between propositions (Dowty 1979:99ff), developing earlier analyses (Dowty 1972, Lewis 1973). In the situation theoretic framework Devlin (1991:186) argues that causation is a fundamental relation in the world linking certain pairs of situations. In the event described in (92) it is clear that for any causal link we posit, both situations involve both the parameters for the acid and the metal.

While there is no clear asymmetry of cause, there is a clear asymmetry of effect: the metal is affected by the dissolution in a way which is intrinsically tied to the temporal structure of the event, as we saw in the previous section. Thus we can solve the linking problem and avoid positing ad hoc that a particular individual is a 'causer.'

On the other hand, it might be argued that the direction of causation is indeed relevant to examples like (92). The NP *the acid* may be analyzed as essentially metonymic for an event or state, so that (92) means something like 'Placing the acid on the metal dissolved the metal' or 'The presence of the acid on the metal dissolved the metal.' Indeed, the fact that the event nominal [*placing the acid on the metal*] or the stative situation nominal [*the presence of the acid on the metal*] can substitute for the NP *the*

---

[17]See however Croft 1991 and Talmy 1985 for two causal approaches which do treat individuals as causes.

acid in (92) suggests the possibility of this analysis. In other words, the intuition some speakers have, of a direction of causation from acid to metal, might reflect the fact that the acid (or perhaps the NP *the acid*) embodies or represents a fuller causal situation. Thus one might explore the possibility of a type-shifting analysis, where the verb *dissolve* selects a situation-denoting element as its subject, coercing an individual into a situation if the subject denotes an individual of the appropriate type.

We might imagine, then, a causation-based argument selection rule placing causers to the left of causees in the argument structure. Without necessarily rejecting this causal analysis, I would like to point out an apparent problem with it. Such a causal rule would make the wrong prediction for verbs of detection such as *monitor* in (93):

(93)   This device monitors the patient's heartbeat.

The object NP *the patient's heartbeat* is an event nominal, and in this case it is this event which is arguably the cause of the monitoring. In any case, there is no monitoring unless there is a causal link from the heartbeat to the device. Thus in a hypothetical situation where the device perfectly simulates the effects of a heartbeat stimulus with no actual connection to the heartbeat, one has the intuition that (93) is false. Similar comments apply to verbs of perception, as in *John saw the cat* or *John saw the cat scratch the sofa*. Here the cat or the sofa-scratching event is necessarily the 'causal origin' of the perception, as discussed in Searle 1984. (At least this is true if we limit ourselves to 'veridical' seeing, i.e., if we ignore non-veridical perception as in *John hit his head and saw stars*, where no actual stars were the origin of John's visual experience.) See the discussion of example (56) above, including the footnote there.

The causal analysis may be workable if such problems can be overcome. But the 'effect'-based view works even in the problematical cases. Verbs of perception like *see*, which are problematical for the causal analysis, are covered by the Notion-Rule, as discussed above. The verb *monitor* might also come under the Notion-Rule, if we accept that the monitoring device is a simple cognitive agent with a 'notion' (i.e. a representation) of the situation being monitored; e.g. in (93) the device would have a notion of the heartbeat. Thus the monitored-thing role is [+nuclear], correctly predicting it to be the object.

Finally, consider verbs like *hit* and *touch*, which do not entail any effect on the object:

(94)   a.   Some hailstones hit the car.
        b.   The cold buckle touched her skin.

The Nuclear Role Rule misses such verbs, since there is no necessary effect on the object. Interestingly, such verbs also do not lend themselves to a causal analysis of the sort outlined above. Note that they do not accept event-denoting subjects:

(95) a. *The falling of the hailstones hit the roof of the car.
      b. *The buckle's contact with her skin touched her skin.

Instead the subject must denote an individual. Thus the problem of identifying a particular participant as a cause arises once again with such verbs. Rather than involving direction of causation, the asymmetry between participants in the *hit* or *touch* relation seems to revolve around some sort of more subtle 'figure-ground' distinction: roughly, the more stationary or permanent item is realized as the object, while the one which moves is realized as the subject, a tendency noted by various researchers including Dowty (1991) (see (19d) and (20d) above). For example, (96a) and (b) are similar in meaning. While either sentence could be used if the car is moving, only (96a) could be used in a situation where the car is stationary.

(96) a. Some hailstones hit the car.
      b. The car hit some hailstones.
      c. The cold buckle touched her skin.
      d. Her skin touched the cold buckle.

Similar comments apply to (96c) and (d). Perhaps we need a new rule to cover these cases, although we will not attempt to formulate this rule here. The point is that the causal analysis does not offer a solution to them. For the time being, then, we will assume the Nuclear Role Rule and leave the causal analysis as a matter for future research.

3 The Part Rule

Our last argument role ordering rule covers verbs which do not involve notions (hence outside the domain of the Notion-Rule) and are stative (hence outside the domain of the Nuclear Role Rule). Among the verbs covered are the so-called 'container verbs' in (97):

(97) a. This toothpaste contains sugar.
      b. The book includes an appendix.

The basic generalization here is that object participant is PART of subject participant ; the primitive PART relation which formed the basis of the mereological theories described above reemerges now in a different context to account for argument selection for these statives.

We state the Part Rule as (98). Whenever the relation denoted by a verb with two arguments x and y necessarily involves x being a PART of y, then x cannot precede y in the roles list.

(98) The Part Rule.

A lexical sign meeting this description is ill-formed:

$$* \quad \begin{bmatrix} \text{RELN} & \boldsymbol{R} \\ \text{ROLES} & <...[\text{ROLE1}]...[\text{ROLE2}]...> \end{bmatrix},$$

where the following lexical entailment holds:
$$\forall x, y \, \Box [\boldsymbol{R} \, (\text{ROLE1}:y, \, \text{ROLE2}:x) \rightarrow PART(\text{WHOLE}:x, \, \text{PART}:y)]$$

For example, in (97a) the sugar is PART of the toothpaste, so sugar cannot be the subject with toothpaste as object, but rather the reverse.

The linguistic term *dominate* is consistent with the Part Rule, since when x dominates y then y is a PART of x.

(99) The VP dominates the NP.

Note there is no transitive verb meaning 'be a constituent of', though such a verb would be useful. For example the verb *constitute* does not mean this, nor does *form* :

(100) a. Twelve men and women constitute/form a jury.
      b. Only three women constituted/formed the jury. #The others were men.

This is predicted by the Part Rule, which rules out such hypothetical verbs. Following is an interesting example from the terminology of unification grammar (Shieber 1986):

(101) a. Feature structure X subsumes feature structure Y.
      b. Feature structure Y extends feature structure X.

These two sentences are synonymous: by definition *subsume* and *extend* are 'lexical doublets', hence a prima facie problem for any theory deriving argument selection from lexical semantics. What is interesting is that assuming the Part Rule, this is an 'exception that proves the rule'. The intuition behind X *extends* Y is that the information in X *includes* the information in Y: if X contains the information 'big and red' and Y contains the information 'big', then X extends Y. The intuition behind Y *subsumes* X is that the set of objects picked out by Y *includes* the set of objects picked out by X: if Y picks out all 'big' things and X picks out all 'big red' things, then Y subsumes X. In other words, the reason why we get lexical doublets for these two relations between feature structures is that inclusion of informational content and inclusion of denotation happen to be inverses when applied to feature structures.

Two examples of terminology from situation semantics are the following.

(102) The situation s involves/ supports the infon i.

Recall that for a situation s to support an infon i means that i is true by virtue of 'internal properties' of s; that is, the truth of i is in some sense contained in s. Once again the argument selection is consistent with the Part Rule since the more inclusive entity is the subject.

The verb *fill* as in (103) is vague between meaning 'cause to completely occupy' as in sentence (a) and 'cause to partially occupy' as in (b):

(103) a. The fire filled the air with smoke.
       b. John filled the doughnut with jelly.

But when the 'theme' role (the role of *smoke* in (a) and *jelly* in (b)) appears as subject, only the 'completely occupy' interpretation is possible:

(104) a. Smoke filled the air.
       b. (*)Jelly filled the doughnut.

Sentence (b) is ruled out by the Part Rule, if this sentence is interpreted so that the jelly is a proper part of the doughnut. Instead it can only mean that jelly permeated the doughnut.

It is possible that the Part Rule can be extended to inclusion of informational content:

(105) This fact entails/ presupposes/ implies/ implicates/ suggests John's claim.

In each case the informational content of 'John's claim' is a PART of the informational content of 'this fact' . The Part Rule predicts this linking pattern, assuming that a quantity of 'information' itself is the semantic content of an NP like *this fact* or *John's claim,* a not unreasonable assumption.

4 Conclusion

In this chapter we have proposed three rules for argument role ordering within the domain of monotransitive verbs: the Notion-Rule; the Nuclear Role Rule; and the Part Rule. We have not retreated to a weaker position using cluster-concepts (as in Dowty 1991) or conceptual structures (as in Jackendoff 1983). The two universal semantic primitives we have employed, NOTION and PART, are firmly grounded in a semantic intuition. Moreover, these semantic primitives are independently needed for an adequate semantics of natural language: the notion of NOTION is needed for an adequate semantics of belief reports (as shown by Crimmins 1989, Crimmins and Perry 1989); and the notion of PART is needed for an adequate semantics of quantity (as argued by Link 1983, Hinrichs 1985, Krifka 1987).

There are three hypothetical types of predicate for which an explicit treatment has not yet been given here. First, there are undoubtedly some 'semantically syncategorematic' verbs which do not fit the structural descriptions of any of the three rules given above (nor any other rule which might be added to our inventory). An example might be *comprise*, as in *The U.S. comprises fifty states.* Secondly, there are some exceptional verbs which fit the structural description of a rule but have the unexpected linking pattern; the examples of *preoccupy* and *concern* are mentioned above. For verbs of both types, the linking pattern must be lexically stipulated. For verbs in the latter class, the lexical stipulation preempts the application of the violated rule. See Chapter 4, section 2 for a more explicit treatment of these two issues.

A third hypothetical type of verb is one which fits the structural descriptions of more than one rule, such that the rules make opposite predictions: that is, one rule prohibits one ordering of the two arguments while the other rule prohibits the reverse ordering. I do not know of any examples of this type, but if such examples are found, then one of two possibilities would be indicated. If there is a tendency for one rule to win out over another (e.g. if the Notion Rule tends to take precedence over the

Nuclear Role Rule), then a hierarchy of rule application would be instituted. But if there are only isolated cases then the linking pattern would simply be lexically stipulated.

Notwithstanding possibilities of this kind, we have managed to treat the argument selection problem for a large class of monotransitives without straying beyond an exceedingly restricted and well-motivated primitive semantic basis, and we have avoided the pitfalls of thematic role type systems, lexical decomposition, and conceptual structures discussed in Chapter 1. Undoubtedly there is much more to say about ordering constraints, but we will leave the issue here. The next step will be to expand our coverage to include ditransitives and oblique complements.

3

Oblique Complements

In the previous chapter we defended a model of argument structure consisting of an ordered list of argument roles.

(106) ROLES $< \rho_1, \ldots \rho_n >$

The arguments of a verb are ordered in a manner consistent with the universal set of ordering constraints applying to the semantics of the verb: the Notion-Rule, the Part Rule, and the Nuclear Role Rule. In this chapter we enhance this minimal structure with a feature $[+r]$ for 'restricted' or oblique roles, i.e. roles which must be linked to a semantically restricted complement such as a PP, semantic case (dative, etc.), or, as we will argue, a semantically restricted NP in some instances.

1 Prepositions and copredication

Consider this puzzle concerning prepositions and the syntactic optionality of arguments ('object deletion'). It is well known that certain arguments of verbs are syntactically optional, and that to some extent this is a matter of lexical stipulation, as shown by well-known contrasts like *John is eating (his peas)* versus *John is devouring *(his peas)*. For example, both the theme and locative arguments of the verb *smear* are syntactically optional, as shown in (107a-d). This optionality might be represented in argument structure with parentheses as in (107e) (ignoring for now the distinction between syntactic and semantic optionality).

(107) a.   Try to avoid smearing the drawing with charcoal.
     b.   Try to avoid smearing the drawing.
     c.   Try to avoid smearing the charcoal.
     d.   Try to avoid smearing.
     e.   smear < agt , (th) , (loc) >

However, when the preposition *with* governs the theme NP *charcoal*, then the goal NP *the drawing* becomes obligatory as well. Compare (107c) to (108).[1]

(108) *Try to avoid smearing with charcoal.

Similarly, the theme *hay* and goal *the trucks* of the verb *load* are both optional (109). But (110a) lacks the implicit goal interpretation, and has only the peculiar reflexive meaning that the men are loading themselves with hay, perhaps like living scarecrows; and (110b) lacks the implicit theme interpretation, and can only mean the men are loading themselves onto the trucks.

(109) a.   Help the men load the trucks with hay.
     b.   Help the men load the trucks.
     c.   Help the men load hay.

(110) a.   (*)Help the men load with hay.
     b.   (*)Help the men load onto the trucks.

In each case there is an implicational relation between the presence of the preposition and the presence of a certain argument of the verb. The preposition not only makes its own object obligatory (which is to be expected) but also makes a particular co-complement obligatory as well. Some further examples follow:

---

[1]This sentence would be acceptable as a label *Do not smear with charcoal* on an item corresponding to the missing argument, e.g. on a drawing. However, labels license omission of otherwise strongly obligatory complements, as in a note on a box of cookies reading *Do not devour.*

(111) a. He refused to tell the story to the authorities.
     b. He refused to tell the story.
     c. He refused to tell the authorities.
     d. He refused to tell.
     e. *He refused to tell to the authorities.

(112) a. The waitress has begun serving dinner to the customers.
     b. The waitress has begun serving the customers.
     c. The waitress has begun serving dinner.
     d. The waitress has begun serving.
     e. ?*The waitress has begun serving to the customers.

(113) a. Shelley fed some oatmeal to Leo.
     b. Shelley fed Leo.
     c. *Shelley fed to Leo.

The complementation patterns above show that apparently syntactic requirements are being imposed by the *preposition* as well as the verb. It is not enough just to indicate optionality in the argument structure of each verb:

(114) a. load < agt , (th) , (loc) >
     b. tell < agt , (rec) , (th) >
     c. feed < agt , rec , (th) >

These fail to explain the ungrammatical examples above.

    This phenomenon can be understood under an analysis of these prepositions as involving *copredication* or argument-sharing (see Gawron 1986). Many prepositions heading complement PPs have semantic content and share certain arguments with the governing verb. Argument sharing can be indicated by coindexing any argument slots of verb and preposition which are both filled by the same entity.

(115) a.   load the truck with hay
     a'. *load* < agt , (th$_i$) , (loc$_j$) > & *with* < loc$_j$, th$_i$ >

    b.   tell the story to the authorities
    b'. *tell* < agt , (rec$_i$) , (th$_j$) > & *to* < rec$_i$, th$_j$ >

    c.   feed the oatmeal to Leo
    c'. *feed* < agt , rec$_i$, (th$_j$) > & *to* < rec$_i$, th$_j$ >

In the same sense that a verb imposes restrictions on optionality of its arguments, a preposition does so as well. If the preposition and verb share an argument then either one may require that the argument be expressed.

    Verb-preposition copredication has been proposed to explain semantically determined preposition selection (Gawron 1986). To take an example from Gawron 1986, a great many of the verbs which select *for*-PPs form a semantic class:

(116) *wish for, hope for, ask for, long for, try for, hunger for, yearn for, strive for, go for...*

Gawron (1986) notes that in every case the object of *for* plays the role of 'object of desire', where the verb indicates the type of desire more specifically (e.g. *hunger for*) or denotes an action which is carried out as a way of attaining the desired goal (*ask for, try for*). In addition, *for*-PPs occur as adjuncts with this same desiderative sense:

(117) a.   Students for a Democratic Society
      b.   John ran for cover when it started to rain.
      c.   John worked for peace.

Gawron argues that a preposition has semantic content, rather than simply tagging a complement of the verb, even when the preposition is uniquely selected by the verb.

    In addition to the distributional evidence above, coordination shows that prepositions such as *for* have semantic content even when marking an argument of a verb. By way of background, consider first of all a very general and clear property of ambiguous phrases: when a single phrase is used simultaneously as a complement of two verbs, it cannot be interpreted in two different senses, one for each verb. A *CD* is either a compact disk or a certificate of deposit, but sentence (118) clearly cannot have the meaning shown.

(118)   *John can't decide whether to listen to or liquidate his CDs.
'John can't decide whether to listen to his compact disks or liquidate his certificates of deposit.'

Actually (118), with the interpretation shown, is marginally acceptable as an instance of *zeugma*, a rhetorical figure used for humorous effect. Here we will confine ourselves to non-figurative speech. We will use this as a diagnostic to test some complement PPs to see whether the preposition has semantic content.[2]

The verbs *search* and *examine* take a 'desiderative' PP[for], representing the thing which is desired; these verbs can be coordinated (119a). Similarly, *praise* and *condemn* take a *for*-PP representing the cause or reason for the praise or condemnation; these can be coordinated (119b). But they cannot be mixed, as shown in (119c).

(119)   a.   They will search and examine George for the letter.
        b.   They will either praise or condemn George for the letter.
        c.   *They will either condemn or search George for the letter.

Some further examples appear in (120) and (121).

(120)   a.   Somehow we must safely pile or cram the weapons into trucks.
        b.   Somehow we must safely transform or convert the weapons into trucks.
        c.   *Somehow we must safely pile or transform the weapons into trucks.

(121)   a.   Tommy's mother sometimes tapes or pins a note to him.
        b.   Tommy's mother sometimes mails or faxes a note to him.
        c.   *Tommy's mother sometimes mails or tapes it to him.

Crucially, there is no injunction against mixing thematic role types in this manner: in (122) Bugsy is the 'agent' of kill but the 'theme' or 'patient' of arrest.

(122)   Bugsy killed someone and was arrested for murder.

---

[2]For our argument it makes no difference whether (118) is analyzed as right node raising or V^0-V^0 coordination.

Similarly, compare failed attempts at coordination like (123a), which resembles the earlier examples, in that the preposition is simultaneously used in two different senses, with relatively better examples like (123b), where the preposition appears twice, once in each sense, so there is no conflict.[3]

(123) a. ??Mikael longed and danced <u>for_{des?/ben?}</u> the Princess of Muu.
   b. Mikael <u>longed for_{des}</u> and <u>danced for_{ben}</u> the Princess of Muu.

If it is not the clash of thematic role types which is responsible for the ungrammaticality of the starred sentences, then it seems that the verbs select for particular senses of P's: *praise* and *condemn* select, not just a PP[for], but a PP[for$_{cause}$], while *search* and *examine* select a PP[for$_{desiderative}$]. Then the contrasts follow automatically from the constraint against (non-figurative) zeugma illustrated by (118) above. Following are some further examples involving the desiderative and benefactive senses of *for*.

(124) a. I wrote this song for Lola. (benefactive)
   b. I wrote this song for money. (desiderative)
   c. *I wrote this song for Lola and money. (des + ben)
   d. Susie went to Stanford for an education. (desiderative)
   e. Susie went to Stanford for her mother. (benefactive)
   f. *Susie went to Stanford for an education and her mother. (des + ben)

The odd sentences (c) and (f) involve an attempt to use a single occurrence of the preposition in two senses, this time because the NP governed by the preposition is a conjoined NP with each conjunct forcing a different preposition sense. Even a fairly idiosyncratic preposition such as the *on* selected by *rely* fails to allow coordinated verbs unless the two preposition meanings are similar:

(125) a. *John relied and concentrated on Mary.
   b. John relied and depended on Mary.

In summary, the evidence given above suggests that prepositions have semantic content, even when they are obligatorily selected by a verb to mark an argument of the verb.

---

[3](123b) may involve V-P incorporation, or perhaps right node raising. As above, this does not affect our argument.

Gawron (1986) proposed that semantically based preposition selection requires that the semantic content of the preposition be a 'component' of the semantic content of the verb.

The preposition *for* occurs with a class of verbs having to do with desire: *wish, hope, pray, ask, long, try, hunger,* and *yearn.* If we posit a relation DESIRE which is a component for all these verbs, and use DESIRE as the lexical relation for one meaning of the preposition *for*, then *for* will be eligible to mark arguments with any of them. The Argument Principle does not require us to do so; it merely licenses the subcategorization as a possible valence for the grammar. (Gawron 1986:344)

The required semantic relation between V and P consists of a necessary constraints like the following (see Chapter 1, section 3 above for an explanation of necessary constraints):

(126) [sl s $\models$ « *YEARN, x, y,* 1 »] $=>_{\{x,y\}}$ [sl s $\models$ « *DESIRE, x, y,* 1 »]

where *YEARN* is the relation denoted by *yearn* and *DESIRE* is the relation denoted by *for* (in the desiderative sense): this constraint says that all yearning (of *x* for *y*) involves desiring (of *x* for *y*). In short the selected preposition is redundant with the verb which semantically selects it, and not meaningless.

As Gawron mentions in the last sentence of the above quote, the proper semantic relation between the lexical meaning of the verb and preposition is a necessary but not sufficient condition for the preposition to be selected for a given complement of the verb. For example the verb *desire* semantically subsumes *for* but fails to select it: **John desired for a job.* Selection is sometimes optional:

(127) a. John sought in vain for a solution.
    b. John sought a solution.

This means that the direct/oblique distinction cannot be derived from the semantics but must be lexically stipulated, at least in some cases.[4]

We will indicate that a role must link to an 'oblique complement', i.e. a thematically restricted complement such as a *for*-PP (rather than a

---

[4]Pinker (1989), inter alia, argues that fine-grained semantic criteria are involved in determining whether a role is realized as direct or oblique (i.e., [+*r*]). See also Wechsler and Lee to appear for a related treatment in terms of case-marking. The present analysis is compatible with such proposals in principle, but they will not be explored here.

simple NP complement) with the feature [+r]. Adopting the terminology of Bresnan and Kanerva 1989, any role with such a feature will be called a *restricted role*.[5] The 'yearned-for' role of *yearn* is a restricted role, while the 'desired' role of *desire* is unrestricted, and the 'sought' role of *seek* is optionally restricted, as indicated by the feature [±r] in (130).

(128) *yearn*
$$\begin{bmatrix} \text{SUBCAT} <...> \\ \text{ROLES} < [\text{YEARNER}], [\text{YEARNED.FOR}]^{[+r]} > \end{bmatrix}$$

(129) *desire*
$$\begin{bmatrix} \text{SUBCAT} <...> \\ \text{ROLES} < [\text{DESIRER}], [\text{DESIRED}] > \end{bmatrix}$$

(130) *seek*
$$\begin{bmatrix} \text{SUBCAT} <...> \\ \text{ROLES} < \text{SEEKER}, \text{SOUGHT}^{[±r]} > \end{bmatrix}$$

Here the superscript [+r] abbreviates the boolean feature RESTRICTED with the value +, so that [YEARNED.FOR]$^{[+r]}$, for example, abbreviates the following:

$$\begin{bmatrix} \text{YEARNED.FOR} & [\,] \\ \text{RESTRICTED} & + \end{bmatrix}$$

The default value for the feature RESTRICTED is minus (–), so this value can be assumed if the + value is not specified.

Now we need a linking principle to link [+r] roles to complements with the appropriate semantics. Our rule must obligatorily link the YEARNED.FOR role of *yearn* and optionally link the SOUGHT role of *seek*, to the desiderative *for*-PP, as shown in (131) and (132) respectively.

---

[5]This notion of *restricted role* should not be confused with *selectional restrictions*. For example, the subject of *saw* in sentences like *1789 saw the abolition of serfdom* must denote a time interval or epoch (a selectional restriction), but it is still [–r]. With a restricted role it is the role itself and not the filler of the role which is semantically restricted.

(131) *yearn*

$$\begin{bmatrix} \text{SUBCAT} < \text{NP}_{[1]}, \text{PP}[for]_{[2]} > \\ \text{ROLES} < [\text{YEARNER}[1]], [\text{YEARNED. FOR}[2]]^{[+r]} > \end{bmatrix}$$

(132) a. *seek*

$$\begin{bmatrix} \text{SUBCAT} < \text{NP}_{[1]}, \text{PP}[for]_{[2]} > \\ \text{ROLES} < [\text{SEEKER}[1]], [\text{SOUGHT}[2]]^{[+r]} > \end{bmatrix}$$

   b. *seek*

$$\begin{bmatrix} \text{SUBCAT} < \text{NP}_{[1]}, \text{NP}_{[2]} > \\ \text{ROLES} < [\text{SEEKER}[1]], [\text{SOUGHT}[2]] > \end{bmatrix}$$

To arrive at a general principle for linking of restricted roles we first need a lexical entry for the (desiderative) preposition *for*. Simplifying somewhat, following is the entry:

(133) *for(des)*

$$\begin{bmatrix} \text{CAT} & \begin{bmatrix} \text{HEAD} & prep \\ \text{SUBCAT} < \text{NP}_{[1]} > \end{bmatrix} \\ \text{CONTENT} & \begin{bmatrix} \text{REL} & desire \\ \text{ROLES} < [\text{DESIRER}], [\text{DESIRED}[1]] > \end{bmatrix} \end{bmatrix}$$

As above we are assuming here that *for* expresses the relation of desire holding between two individuals; the DESIRED role is filled by the NP which the preposition subcategorizes for ('NP$_{[1]}$'), that is, the object of the preposition. We abbreviate (133) by underlining the relevant role as in (134).

(134) P$_{for}$[desire< desirer, desired >]

The underlining is an abbreviatory convention to indicate that this is the argument linked to the (sole) subcategorized complement; we will call this the *distinguished argument role* of the preposition. Thus (135) represents a phrase XP expressing the relation R' with a distinguished argument role p:

(135) XP[R'<...p...>]

With this convention in place let us formulate our restricted linking principle. The principle should say the following: any [+r] role must be linked to a complement phrase with semantic content bearing the appropriate relation to the verb's semantic content. The constraint in (134) does this by saying that any restricted verb role (V-ROLE$^{[+r]}$) must be linked to a phrase (XP) such that the verb-denoted relation (R) and the XP-denoted relation (R') are connected by the entailment shown.

(136) Restricted Linking Principle.

$$\begin{bmatrix} \text{CAT} & [\text{HEAD } verb] \\ \text{CONTENT} & \begin{bmatrix} \text{REL} & V\text{-}REL \\ \text{ROLES} & <...\,V\text{–ROLE}^{[+r]}...> \end{bmatrix} \end{bmatrix} \Rightarrow$$

$$\begin{bmatrix} \text{CAT} & [\text{SUBCAT} <...\,\text{XP}[P\text{–}REL <...[\underline{\text{P–ROLE}}\,[1]]...>]...>] \\ \text{CONTENT} & [\text{ROLES} \quad <...[\text{V–ROLE}\,[1]]^{[+r]}...>] \end{bmatrix}$$

where this entailment holds:
$$\forall x\, \square\,[V\text{-}REL(...V\text{-ROLE}:x...) \rightarrow P\text{-}REL(...P\text{-ROLE}:x...)]$$

The Restricted Linking Principle states that for restricted linking to occur there must be some entailment involving the argument role V-ROLE of the verb and the argument slot P-ROLE of the PP or other restricted complement. Our rule identifies slot P-ROLE as the designated argument slot of the complement (as notated by the underlining that role within the subcat list item XP[P-REL <... P-ROLE ...>]); and it identifies slot V-ROLE of the verb as the argument role we are interested in linking. Thus the sort of entailment which must hold involves the verb and the copredicator sharing (at least) that designated and semantically linked argument. It could also involve sharing other arguments, but minimally the one argument linked to the restricted complement must be shared.

As an example, consider the *to*-PP selected by the verbs in (137).

(137) a.   John donated/contributed/gave books to the library.
       b.   John mailed/sent books to the library.

I assume that these verbs have three argument roles, of which the recipient role is restricted:

(138) *donate*
       [ROLES < AGT, REC$^{[+r]}$, TH >]

The semantic content of the preposition *to* is a three-place relation *INT.CAUSE.REC* ('<u>int</u>end to <u>cause</u> to <u>rec</u>eive') which holds between three individuals x, y, and z just in case x is an intentional agent (filling slot *ag*) who carries out an action with the intention that that action cause y (filling slot *rec*) to receive z (filling slot *th*).

(139) *to(recip)*
       P[INT.CAUSE.REC < ag:x, <u>rec:y</u>, th:z >]

This relation will be discussed further below. The recipient role *rec* is the designated argument slot for this preposition, since the object of *to* fills that slot. The relation expressed only involves y being the *intended* recipient, not necessarily the actual one; evidence is the interpretation of adjunct *to*-PPs:

(140) a message to Mary
       = 'a message intended for Mary'
       ≠ 'a message which Mary received'

For each of the verbs in (137) a necessary constraint of the requisite form holds between the verb and the preposition. Take *donate* for example:

(141) $\forall x,y,z$ [*DONATE*(ag:x, rec:y, th:z) →
       INT.CAUSE.REC(ag:x, rec:y, th:z)]

In prose, this says: in donating (e.g.) books to the library, the donor carries out an action with the intention that this action will cause the library to receive the books. Indeed the relation between *donate* and *to* indicated in (141) is considerably tighter than what is necessary to link the recipient of *donate* with a *to*-PP, given the Restricted Linking Principle. In particular, all three arguments of *donate* are shared: agent, recipient, and theme; while it is only required that the designated argument of *to* (the recipient) be shared.

It also happens that *donate, contribute,* and *give* (as well as *sell, loan,* and numerous other verbs of possession transfer) entail a relation stronger than *INT.CAUSE.REC*: not only must the agent intend that the event cause the recipient to receive the theme, the event must *actually* cause the recipient to receive the theme; i.e. the agent's intentions must be fulfilled.

But the weaker entailment (141) needed to select *to* is also satisfied. The verbs *mail* and *send* (as in 137b) do not have this stronger entailment: one can mail or send books books to the library without the books reaching their intended destination. For these verbs the entailment needed for selecting a *to*-PP still holds:

(142) $\forall x,y,z$ [*SEND*(ag:x, rec:y, th:z) $\rightarrow$

$\quad\quad$ *INT.CAUSE.REC*(ag:x, rec:y, th:z)]

By the Restricted Linking Principle each of these verbs links the recipient role to a *to*-PP.

(143) linking the recipient role of *donate, send,* etc.

$$\begin{bmatrix} \text{CAT} & \begin{bmatrix} \text{HEAD } verb \\ \text{SUBCAT } <...\text{PP}[to]_{[1]}...> \end{bmatrix} \\ \text{CONTENT} & \begin{bmatrix} \text{RELN } R \\ \text{ROLES} < \text{AG},[\text{REC } [1]]^{[+r]}, \text{TH} > \end{bmatrix} \end{bmatrix}$$

The remainder of the linking follows from general principles: being unrestricted, the agent and theme roles must link to NP complements; by the Isomorphy Constraint the lines of association cannot cross; and by conditions on SUBCAT lists NPs are less oblique than PPs.

(144) *donate, send,* etc.

$$\begin{bmatrix} \text{CAT} & \begin{bmatrix} \text{HEAD } verb \\ \text{SUBCAT } < \text{NP}_{[1]}, \text{NP}_{[2]}, \text{PP}[to]_{[3]} > \end{bmatrix} \\ \text{CONTENT} & \begin{bmatrix} \text{RELN } R \\ \text{ROLES} < [\text{AG}[1]],[\text{REC}[3]]^{[+r]},[\text{TH}[2]] > \end{bmatrix} \end{bmatrix}$$

By the general syntactic principles of HPSG (see Chapter 1, section 3 above) the subcat list items are cancelled from right to left; the NP$_{[2]}$ and PP[*to*] are cancelled first, and so are sisters to V under VP; the unmarked linear order of sister complements follows the subcat order (see (28)); and finally the subject NP$_{[1]}$ is added to the VP to form a saturated clause. The result is the sentence in (137) with the correct interpretation.

We look at verbs of this class in more detail in the next section. Consider now cases of idiosyncratic preposition selection:

(145) Dan interested Mary in wolves.
       (cp. *Dan fascinated/intrigued/thrilled Mary in wolves.)

The preposition *in* is lexically subcategorized by the verb *interest*. I will assume that this role is not restricted (not [+r]), but rather that the selection of *in* is specified in the lexical entry for *interest*.

(146) *interest*
$$\begin{bmatrix} \text{SUBCAT} < ...\text{PP}[in]_{[3]}...> \\ \text{ROLES} <[\text{AG}[1]],[\text{EXP}[2]],[\text{TH}[3]]> \end{bmatrix}$$

As above, the rest of the linking follows from general principles: the agent and experiencer are unrestricted, so they link to NPs; by the Isomorphy constraint the linking cannot cross; and syntactic constraints on the subcat list specify that NPs are less oblique than PPs.

(147) *interest*
$$\begin{bmatrix} \text{SUBCAT} < \text{NP}_{[1]},\text{NP}_{[2]},\text{PP}[in]_{[3]} > \\ \text{ROLES} <[\text{AG}[1]],[\text{EXP}[2]],[\text{TH}[3]]> \end{bmatrix}$$

To summarize, we have proposed that verb roles are linked to PPs in two sorts of cases: (i) when they are marked [+r] and the verb meaning subsumes the head preposition's meaning; and (ii) when a preposition is idiosyncratically selected by the verb to mark a given role. In the next section we argue that along with its semantically restricted PP complements, English has certain semantically restricted NP complements.

2 The restricted recipient NP

A pervasive and well-known property of English ditransitives (148a, 149a) is that the inner object almost always plays the role of *recipient* of the individual denoted by the outer object NP (Green 1974, Oehrle 1976, Pinker 1989, Wechsler 1991).

(148) a. Fred gave/sent/mailed/served Mary the cookies.
     b. Fred gave/sent/mailed/served the cookies to Mary.

(149) a. Emma TeXed (Mary) a document.
     b. Emma TeXed a document (for Mary).

There are no ditransitives with an inner object instrumental, for example:

(150) *John chopped the ax the tree.

More precisely, in the interpretation of the sentences in (148a) and (149a) an agent performs an action on an individual z with the intention that y receive z. We have posited a three-place relation *INT.REC(x,y,z)* which holds just in case an agent x (filling the *ag* slot) performs an action on an individual z (filling the *th* slot) with the intention that y (filling the *rec* slot) receive z. We will use this abbreviation:

(151) NP[*int.rec*] abbreviates NP[*INT.REC* < ag:*x*, int.rec:*y*, th:*z* >]

We can express the generalization about English ditransitives by associating the *int.rec* relation with the second NP in the subcat list.

(152) *English verb subcat lists.* (X≠N)
     [SUBCAT < NP, (NP[*int.rec*],) (Prt,) (NP,) XP* >]

This list represents the total set of possible subcat lists, from which each English verb's list is taken. (Or a single list into which each English verb's list is embedded.) Most of the constraints determining which of these possible lists is the actual one for a given verb are derived from argument structure and general principles of linking, but there are a few syntactic restrictions on subcat lists to be discussed below, viz. all passive verbs lack NP[*int.rec*] and certain actives such as *donate* lack both NP[*int.rec*] and the particle (Prt).

     The first NP in the list is the subject, and the next two NPs appear in the order of obliqueness, due to this LP rule given in (28) above (cp. Pollard and Sag 1987):

(153) LP rule:
     COMPLEMENT$_1$ < COMPLEMENT$_2$
     where COMPLEMENT$_1$ is less oblique than COMPLEMENT$_2$

As a result the NP[*int.rec*] always appears in the immediately post-verbal position:

(154)

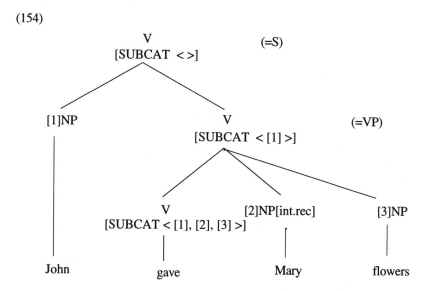

One can therefore think of this NP[*int.rec*] as a phrase structure position. The notion of thematically restricted phrase structure positions is familiar from GB under the rubric of *inherent Case* i.e. abstract Case inherently associated with a specific θ-role, and plays an important role in LMT, where one of the four basic grammatical functions is the *restricted object* ([+r,+o]).[6]

Semantically the recipient NP resembles a complement PP, which turns out to be virtually synonymous with one meaning of the *for*-PP (not the *to*-PP as commonly supposed). Both 'recipient' *for* and the inner object NP denote the relation we have named *int.rec*, while the *to* of possession denotes the relation we have named *int.cause.rec:*

---

[6]Neither theory has been applied to this problem in the way I do here, as far as I know. See however Smith 1992 for a treatment similar to the present one, supported by considerable independent cross-linguistic evidence.

(155) a. 'recipient' *for* and NP[*int.rec*]:
           INT.REC(x,y,z) holds between three individuals *x, y,* and *z* just in
           case *x* performs an action on *z* with the intention that *y* receive *z*.

       b. 'recipient' *to:*
           INT.CAUSE.REC(x,y,z,e) holds between three individuals *x, y,*
           and *z* just in case *x* performs an action with the intention that an
           action cause *y* to receive *z*.

Note first of all that both relations involve intentions and not necessarily
actual fulfillment of those intentions, a matter to which we return below.
The two relations differ however in that *int.cause.rec* involves (intended)
causation while *int.rec* does not, as illustrated by the difference in
interpretation between (156a) and (b), and the oddity of (c).

(156) a. John baked a cake for Mary.
           'John baked a cake with the intention that Mary receive it.'
       b. John mailed a cake to Mary.
           'John mailed a cake with the intention that mailing the cake
           cause Mary to receive it.'
       c. *John baked a cake to Mary.
           (odd because baking a cake cannot *cause* Mary to receive it)

The *for*-datives (ditransitives which alternate with *for*-phrases) will be
discussed further in section 3 below. For now let us consider linking for the
to-dative verbs such as *give* and *mail*.

Notice first of all that the *int.cause.rec* relation involves (is more
specific than) the *INT.REC* relation; that is, intending that an action cause *y*
to receive *z* involves (at least) intending that *y* receive *z*. Thus both of
these entailments hold:

(157) a. $\forall x,y,z \; [GIVE(\text{ag}:x, \text{rec}:y, \text{th}:z)] \rightarrow$
           $INT.CAUSE.REC(\text{ag}:x, \text{rec}:y, \text{th}:z)]$
       b. $\forall x,y,z \; [GIVE(\text{ag}:x, \text{rec}:y, \text{th}:z) \rightarrow$
           $INT.REC \; (\text{ag}:x, \text{rec}:y, \text{th}:z)]$

As noted above, the verb *give* happens to be stronger, entailing not only
intended but *actual* receiving, but the weaker constraints in (157) are also
true. Thus the recipient role of a *to*-dative verb can link to either a *to*-PP or
the NP[*int.rec*], the source of the dative alternation:

(158) a. John gave the children the books.
give
$$\begin{bmatrix} \text{SUBCAT} < \text{NP}_{[1]}, \text{NP}[\textit{int. rec}]_{[2]}, \text{NP}_{[3]} > \\ \text{ROLES} < [\text{AG}[1]], [\text{REC}[2]]^{[+r]}, [\text{TH}[3]] > \end{bmatrix}$$

b. John gave the books to the children.
give
$$\begin{bmatrix} \text{SUBCAT} < \text{NP}_{[1]}, \text{NP}_{[3]}, \text{PP}[\textit{to}]_{[2]} > \\ \text{ROLES} < [\text{AG}[1]], [\text{REC}[2]]^{[+r]}, [\text{TH}[3]] > \end{bmatrix}$$

An unsolved question is why the recipient of *give* cannot link to a *for*-PP as in **John gave the books for the children* (meaning 'to the children'). This could involve a sort of elsewhere condition, which states that the option with the more restrictive environmental specification must be chosen (cp. the Restrictiveness Condition of Smith 1992). To prevent the Restrictiveness Condition from incorrectly ruling out the dative shift itself, we would have to assume that the restricted NP is ambiguous between *INT.CAUSE.REC* and *INT.REC*. We will not pursue this matter further here.

To account for passive (and certain other facts to be discussed below) let us assume that the [+r] feature on the recipient is optional. We adopt a suppression (demotion) account of the passive (inter alia Kiparsky 1987, Bresnan and Kanerva 1989). In the passive form *given* the highest role is suppressed, which we indicate with the feature [*sup*]:

(159) a. active: give
[ROLES < AG , REC$^{[\pm r]}$, TH >]

b. passive: give+EN
[ROLES < AG[*sup*], REC$^{[\pm r]}$, TH >]

The giver role is semantically filled but the individual filling it is either linguistically unexpressed or expressed in a by-phrase PP[*by, sup*], which is restricted to linking (otherwise) suppressed arguments. More generally, the passive affix signifies that the highest (i.e. leftmost) role is suppressed.

(160) passive morpheme.
-en$_\text{v}$
[ROLES < [*sup*] , ... >]

In many dialects of English the NP[*int.rec*] option is not available in the passive, the so-called 'case absorption' phenomenon (see Chomsky 1981), which prevents the theme from passivizing in the presence of the recipient NP:

(161) %The books were given the children. (dialect)

For the 'American English' dialect which rejects (161), we must further stipulate that English passive verbs lack NP[*int.rec*] in their subcat lists:

(162) English passive morpheme (X≠N):   ('American' dialect)
       $-en_V$

$$\begin{bmatrix} \text{SUBCAT} & < \text{NP},(\text{Pr t}),(\text{NP}),\text{XP*} > \\ \text{ROLES} & < [sup],...> \end{bmatrix}$$

Case absorption is not a universal component of passive, indeed in Scandinavian (see Åfarli 1989a,b, and section 6 below) and some dialects of English the theme may be passivized over the recipient NP as in (161). In such dialects and languages the passive is simply (160) above.

   Linking of passive verbs follows the same general principles (Isomorphy Condition, Restricted Linking Condition) as linking of actives. In the variant of *given* with the [+*r*] recipient, the recipient can only be linked by a *to*-PP, since NP[*int.rec*] is not available.

(163) The books were given to the children by John.
       given

$$\begin{bmatrix} \text{SUBCAT} & < \text{NP}_{[3]},\text{PP}[to]_{[2]},\text{PP}[by]_{[1]} > \\ \text{ROLES} & < [\text{AG}[1]][sup],[\text{REC}[2]]^{[+r]},[\text{TH}[3]] > \end{bmatrix}$$

In the variant with [−r] on the recipient, the recipient must be linked by an unrestricted NP (and anyway no restricted NP is available since it is a passive form), hence the recipient must emerge as the subject:

(164) The children were given the books (by John).
       given

$$\begin{bmatrix} \text{SUBCAT} & < \text{NP}_{[2]},\text{NP}_{[3]},\text{PP}[by]_{[1]} > \\ \text{ROLES} & < [\text{AG}[1]][sup],[\text{REC}[2]],[\text{TH}[3]] > \end{bmatrix}$$

The distribution of the particle provides independent evidence for the disappearance of the restricted NP in passives (Kiparsky 1988):

(165) a.   We sent (*right) up a drink.
     b.   We sent a drink (right) up.
     c.   We sent John (*right) up a drink.
     d.   John was sent (*right) up a drink.
     e.   *John was sent a drink up.

Following Emonds 1976 and Sag 1985 I assume that *up* in (165a,c,d) is a particle while *up* in (165b) is an intransitive PP, as shown by the acceptability of the PP-modifier *right* in the latter but not the former case. A PP analysis of *up* in (165e) is unavailable because directional PPs are incompatible with recipients more generally: *?*We sent John a letter to Texas; *John was sent a drink to his room.* But the question is why the particle analysis of *up* is not available in (165e). The disappearance of NP[*int.rec*] in the passive explains this. Since the restricted NP[*int.rec*] is the only NP (other than the subject) which is less oblique than the particle (< NP, (NP[*int.rec*]), (Prt), (NP),... >) the unacceptability of (165e) provides independent evidence that the restricted NP[*int.rec*] is unavailable in the passive. (Further evidence is given below.)

    In addition, a number of English active verbs lack both NP[*int.rec*] and the particle (Prt), as illustrated in (166) and (167) respectively (see Di Sciullo and Williams 1987):

(166)   *John donated/distributed/contributed the homeless people his money.
       (cp. John donated/distributed/contributed his money to the homeless people

(167) a.   *John donated away his money.
        (cp. John gave away his money.)
     b.   *John distributed out his money.
        (cp. John handed out his money.)
     c.   *John contributed in his money.
        (cp. John added in his money.)

As with the passive verbs, the verbs of the *donate* type have a slightly restricted range of subcategorized complements.

    The semantic range of ditransitive constructions is slightly broader than we have so far suggested, but falls into the following closely related semantic classes (see Goldberg 1992 for a more detailed account of these types).

(168) a. *give, hand, serve, feed,...*
   b. *throw, toss, kick, poke, fling, shoot, bring, take, bequeath, leave, allocate, reserve, grant,...*
   c. illocutionary act: *promise, guarantee,...*
   d. acts of permission: *permit, allow, ...*
   e. negated version of c or d: *refuse, deny...*
   f. communication: *tell, ...*
   g. concealed questions (Baker 1968): *She asked Sam a question/ his name/ his marital status.*
   h. event nominal for theme: *She gave him a wink/ a kick/ etc.*

These various interpretations of the ditransitive are nearly all semantically very close to the relation *INT.REC*, i.e. the performance of an act by x with the intention that y receive z.   The verb types (168a) and (168b) have already been discussed. The (c) and (d) verbs also involve *INT.REC*, but it happens that the actions taken (with the intention that y receive z) are illocutionary acts (c) or acts of permission (d). (168e) are negated version of (c) or (d). (168f) involve the intention that y receive some information z; (168g) do not involve receiving but they may be extensions of (168f); and (168h) are metaphorical extensions of the notion of receiving ('receiving a kick').

There are almost no ditransitives in English for which the inner object is not an 'intended recipient' or a close extension of that role. One exception is *envy:*

(169) (%)I envy John his good looks.

(Some speakers have only the monotransitive valence for *envy.*) This verb is treated as analogous to the idiosyncratic (non-semantic) preposition selection (cp. the treatment of *rely on* above), that is, the linking for the envied-person role is stipulated in the lexical entry. Otherwise, it is a striking fact that there are no ditransitives with other roles played by the inner object:

(170) *John chopped the ax the tree.

There are no verbs taking an instrumental inner object in English. This fact is immediately explained on the present account, since for us the subcat list item corresponding to the inner object NP (i.e. the second NP on the list) is semantically restricted.

Some *for*-dative ditransitives which (we argue) involve recipients which are semantic adjuncts (as discussed in the next section) are given in (171a); some metaphorical extensions are in (171b).

(171) Adjunct uses.
    a.   *paint, build, fricassee, TeX, carve, ...*
    b.   extentions: *Cry me a river, Slay me a dragon, ...* (cp. **Cross me the ocean.*)[7]

The restriction to the recipient interpretation can also be seen by observing the sort of *for*-PP which alternate with the ditransitive form.

(172) a.   John taught the syntax class for Mary.
     a'. *John taught Mary the syntax class.
     b.   John crossed the ocean for Mary.
     b'. *John crossed Mary the ocean.
     c.   John painted a picture for Mary.
     c'. John painted Mary a picture.

See inter alia Gropen et al 1989. *for*-PPs which alternate with the ditransitive form do not include the deputive *for*, where an action that was supposed to have been performed by one person is performed by a different person instead, to benefit the first person. Instead, only the recipient type can appear in the ditransitive (172c), as predicted since this is precisely the semantic content of the NP[*int.rec*] complement.[8]

---

[7]In e.g. *Lancelot will slay her a dragon* Lancelot slays the dragon as a demonstration of his love, but does not intend that she literally receive the slain dragon. Still, these are considerably worse if the second object refers to something which lacks even the *potential* of being received, such as something filling a path role: **Lancelot will cross me an ocean.* Perhaps the slain dragon which is the end-product of the action can symbolize his devotion, while there is no comparable end-product of crossing an ocean (cp. *this (slain) dragon is for you!/*this (crossed) ocean is for you!*).

[8]The dative is better if the second object referent is merely transformed than if it ceases to exist altogether:

(i)   (?)John melted his mother some ice cubes.
(ii)   *John ate his mother some spinach.

What is received in (i) is of course not ice cubes but water; but in (ii) there is nothing available to be received.

Notice that our account does not involve any dativizing 'rule' at any level of grammar; the two alternants in the dative alternation reflect two options for linking, given the similar semantic contents of the complements themselves: the *to*-PP (*INT.CAUSE.REC*) and the inner object NP (*INT.REC*). Thus we 'dissolve' the problem put forth by Pinker (1989): why should a dativization rule observe any semantic constraints at all? (see also Gropen et al 1989) For us the semantic constraints follow from the semantics of the subcat list items themselves, and there is no dativization rule.

Next we look in more detail at the '*for*-datives', i.e. the inner objects alternating with *for*-PPs as in (172c).

3 Valency and *for*-datives

The assumption of a restricted recipient NP also provides an explanation for the behaviour of English benefactive phrases illustrated in (173):

(173) a. Fred carved (Mary) a statue.
     a'. Fred carved a statue (for Mary).

     b. Fred steamed (Mary) some clams.
     b'. Fred steamed some clams (for Mary).

The benefactive alternation poses a dilemma for theories of the semantic valency of predicates, since intuitively carving (e.g.) is not a triadic relation between a carver, a thing-carved, and recipient or benefactive, but only a dyadic relation between a carver and a thing-carved.

Such semantic considerations suggest that the benefactive phrase is an *adjunct,* both in the ditransitive construction (173a,b) and the *for*-PP (173a',b'). There is no semantic justification for considering the recipients to be arguments of the verbs, unless we stretch the notion of 'argument' to the point of vacuity. It is difficult to find even a single proposed *semantic* test for argumenthood which these benefactives pass (syntactic tests are a different matter, as we will see shortly).

First of all, Jackendoff (1990), who argues on independent grounds that these are adjuncts, points out that the benefactive is always optional, and there is no conceivable reason why they should be part of the semantics of a verb like *make* or *carve*. *for*-datives are not 'ontologically necessary' for the denoted events in question, so they fail one suggested criterion for argumenthood (Pollard and Sag 1987:132). One can simply carve something without intending that anyone receive it.

Secondly, these *for*-datives make a uniform contibution to semantic content across a broad range of verbs, another semantic adjunct property (Pollard and Sag 1987:136). That contribution is precisely the relation *INT.REC* (see (155) above). *for*-datives appear on any verb with which they are semantically compatible, i.e. roughly any verb denoting an event involving an intentional agent and some object capable of being received; indeed such broad distribution has been proposed as a property of adjuncts (Huddleston 1984)

Third, Moravcsik (1990:246ff) has proposed that arguments correspond to those participants that enter into the *persistence* and *individuation* conditions of the event; these *for*-recipients have neither property. If they were part of the *persistence* conditions this would mean the following: we would consider that *two distinct carving events* had occurred if Fred carved a single statue, but began carving it with Susan in mind as the statue's eventual recipient, changed his mind half-way through and decided to give it to Mary. But in fact one has the intuition that it is a single carving event, so by that criterion Susan and Mary are filling adjunct roles and not argument roles. (By contrast, both Fred and the statue come out as arguments: if the carver changes halfway through then one could plausibly break this event into two distinct carving events, one per carver; likewise if Fred carves two statues.) If the recipients were crucial to *individuation* conditions, this would mean that if Fred carved a statue with both Mary and Susan in mind as eventual recipients, then he would be engaged in two distinct actions at once. Again, this seems to be an implausible notion of event or action. (By contrast, if two carvers worked together, one could plausibly break this down into two carving situations, one per carver; likewise if Fred carves two statues at once.) Admittedly these tests are vague and difficult to apply with certainty, but in any case they do not clearly point to the benefactive participant being an argument.

Fourth, there are no lexical idiosyncracies of the sort found, for example, with optional agent roles:

(174) break < (ag), th >
   a. The vase broke.
   b. John broke the vase.

(175) fall < th >
   a. The vase fell.
   b. *John fell the vase.

(176) disappear < th >
    a. The rabbit disappeared.
    b. *The magician disappeared the rabbit.

(177) vanish < th >
    a. My wallet seems to have vanished mysteriously.
    b. *Someone apparently vanished my wallet.

The agent role is semantically compatible with *fall, disappear,* and *vanish,* but happens not to be an option, as shown in (175-177), suggesting that the agent is an argument. But I have not been able to find a single English verb for which the *for*-recipient is semantically compatible but nevertheless disallowed. This casts doubt on the view that verbs like *bake* (as in *John baked (Mary) some cookies*) have argument structures with an optional recipient, like the following: <ag (rec) th>. If the information about the recipient role were recorded in individual lexical entries, then nothing would prevent the existence of some verbs which idiosyncratically lack the recipient role, just as we find verbs which reject the agent in the causative transitives. The absence of such lexical idiosyncracies suggests a more general explanation for the optional recipient: either it is an adjunct, or it is an argument added by an exceptionless lexical valence-increasing rule. The lexical rule analysis will be discussed and rejected below (section 5).

    Fifth, *for*-recipients and inner-object recipients can iterate, a property of adjuncts, and not arguments like those in (d)-(f) ((d) and (e) are from Pollard and Sag 1987:136):[9]

(178) a. John bought his aunt some diapers yesterday for the new baby.
    b. John bought her these for the new baby.
    c. John bought some diapers for his aunt for the new baby.
    d. *Chris rented the gazebo to yuppies, to libertarians.
    e. *Josh longed for a gas-guzzler, for a Buick.
    f. *Chris rented some yuppies the gazebo to libertarians.

Each of the sentences (a)-(c) allows an interpretation with two recipients; indeed this is probably the most prominent reading (a deputive reading is possible in (c), where John buys the diapers on his aunt's behalf but not

---

[9]As predicted, it is impossible to get two inner object recipients, since there is only one restricted NP[*int.rec*]:

(i)   *John bought his aunt the new baby some diapers yesterday.

with her in mind as recipient). The adverb *yesterday* in (a) and the use of *these* in (b) prevent the [NP PP]$_{NP}$ analysis, e.g. [some diapers for the new baby]$_{NP}$; cp. *[these for the new baby]$_{NP}$.

Sentences with two (recipient) *for*-PPs like (178c) are slightly awkward, but no worse than double PPs on NPs like the following.

(179) [diapers for my aunt for the baby]$_{NP}$

Clearly these PP modifiers are adjuncts, so if the PPs in (178c) were arguments, we would expect a contrast: the PPs in (178c) should sound worse than those in (175); but in fact they are no worse. (See Johnston 1992 for discussion.)

While the *for*-recipients have the semantic properties of adjuncts, they have most of the syntactic properties of complements, with some crucial exceptions to be discussed below. An obvious complement property is that they can be expressed by the immediately post-verbal NP, which is otherwise assumed to be a subcategorized complement.

Also, there is evidence that the recipient *for*-PPs are dominated by VP, assuming the structure in (180c) (Johnston 1992).

(180) a. What John did was make a bomb for George. for.recip/ for.please
      b. What John did for George was make a bomb. *for.recip/ for.please
      c. What NP did... was VP.

Johnston (1992) distinguishes the *for* of 'pleasing' from the *for* of receiving; he points out that sentences like (180a) are ambiguous: John could have made the bomb with George in mind as the recipient but not necessarily the beneficiary (e.g. if George is the target of the bombing) or as the beneficiary (e.g. if he is providing the bomb to George for George to use on someone else). But (180b) is unambiguous, allowing only the for.please reading. This follows if the *for*-PP of receiving is generated under the VP, while the *for* of pleasing is under S.

(181) a. What John did was [make a bomb for George]$_{VP}$.   for.recip
      a'. What John did was [make a bomb]$_{VP}$ for George.   for.please
      b. What John did for George was [make a bomb]$_{VP}$.
            *for.recip/ for.please

To summarize, *for*-datives have the semantic properties of adjunct roles but the syntactic properties of complement phrases.

The solution to this dilemma which I propose is that these recipients are expressed as complements, but are 'adjunct roles' which have been added to the verb's valence in accordance with the universal condition that verb valence may be increased only in one of two ways:

> (i) by a *morpholexical operation* (an 'affix-mediated' operation, in the terminology of Marantz 1984) such as applicativization (in e.g. Bantu), relational preverb cliticization (Craig and Hale 1988) or preposition-incorporation (in e.g. Swedish; see (198) below); or

> (ii) by linking adjunct roles to *thematically restricted complements* such as PPs or, in the case of English ditransitives, the restricted NP[*int.rec*].

This means that certain roles— necessarily roles for which thematically restricted complements exist— may have the semantic properties of adjuncts and the syntactic properties of complements.

The English benefactive 'shift' is not a morpholexical operation, as there is no applicative morpheme on the verb. Instead, English *for*-datives, I will claim, are of the latter type: they are roles optionally added to verbs, an option allowed in this instance because the *for*-datives are linked to a semantically restricted complement. The semantically restricted complements of English, shown in (178b), are the PPs (those with semantic content, excluding the idiosyncratically selected PPs and passive *by*-phrases) and of course the special 'dative' NP[*int.rec*]:[10]

(182) *English subcat list items.*
     a.   Unrestricted: NP
                               $PP_{by}[sup]$
     b.   Restricted: NP[*int.rec*],
                               $PP_{to}[int.cause.rec]$,
                               $PP_{for}[int.rec]$,
                               $PP_{with}[instrument]$,
                               etc.

We will implement this proposal by requiring that any adjunct roles (ADJ.ROLES) added to a verb's lexical entry must be [+r]. The recipient *Mary* in (183), which is an ADJ.ROLE of the verb *carve,* is linked to the restricted NP in (a) and the restricted PP_{for} in (b), so both are allowed.

---

[10]Since the preposition *by*-phrases impose no thematic restrictions (cp. non-agentive *by*-phrases as in *The vowel is preceded by a consonant*), we assume that the *by*-phrase is [–r].

(183) a. John carved Mary a statue.

carve

$$\left[\begin{array}{ll} \text{CAT} & \left[\begin{array}{l} \text{HEAD } \textit{verb} \\ \text{SUBCAT } <...\text{NP}[\textit{int. rec}]_{[2]}...> \end{array} \right] \\ \\ \text{CONTENT} & \left[\begin{array}{ll} \text{RELN} & \text{carve} \\ \text{ROLES} & <[\text{AGT}], [\text{TH}]> \\ \text{ADJ–ROLES} & <[\text{REC}[2]]^{[+r]}> \end{array} \right] \end{array} \right]$$

b. John carved a statue for Mary.

carve

$$\left[\begin{array}{ll} \text{CAT} & \left[\begin{array}{l} \text{HEAD } \textit{verb} \\ \text{SUBCAT } <...\text{PP}[\textit{for; int. rec}]_{[2]}...> \end{array} \right] \\ \\ \text{CONTENT} & \left[\begin{array}{ll} \text{RELN} & \text{carve} \\ \text{ROLES} & <[\text{AGT}],[\text{TH}]> \\ \text{ADJ–ROLES} & <[\text{REC}[2]]^{[+r]}> \end{array} \right] \end{array} \right]$$

(For simplicity I have omitted the linking of the agent and theme roles.)

We can state this restriction by disallowing unrestricted ([–r]) adjunct roles:

(184) Contraint on Adjunct Roles.
       *[ADJ.ROLES <...[–r]...>]

This rules out adjuncts in unrestricted 'positions', e.g. in subject position or in an unrestricted object position; but it allows adjunct recipients in the inner object 'position' because that position is semantically restricted.

According to our analysis, adjunct roles such as the *for*-recipient roles are not subcategorized by the verb. Instead they can be freely added, as long as they are restricted ([+r]). However, the restricted complement to which they link effectively determines their role by adding a piece of semantics (here the relation *INT.REC*), and this restricts the distribution of the adjunct to certain verbs since it will be semantically compatible only with certain verbs.

Next we will look at evidence for this account.

4 Predictions of the account

Our account predicts first of all that *for*-dative ditransitives will be harder to passivize than *to*-dative ditransitives, which is true:

(185) a.   *He was sanded a board by the carpenter.
      b.   He was handed a board by the carpenter.
      c.   *I'd like to be ground up some coffee.
      d.   I'd like to be sent up some coffee.

Indeed, this contrast has in fact long been noted (Fillmore 1965, Green 1974, Oehrle 1976). This is predicted because the subject NP is unrestricted, so by the Contraint on Adjunct Roles (184) and the Restricted Linking Principle, an adjunct cannot be linked to it. In the passive forms in (185a) and (c) the highest role (the agent) is suppressed, and the recipient, being an adjunct, is necessarily $[+r]$ and therefore cannot link to an unrestricted complement (by the Restricted Linking Principle); thus we predict that the only role which can serve as subject is the theme. This is true, as seen in (187).

(186)   *sanded (passive)*

$$
\begin{bmatrix}
\text{CAT} & \begin{bmatrix} \text{HEAD } \textit{verb} \\ \text{SUBCAT} <...> \end{bmatrix} \\[3ex]
\text{CONTENT} & \begin{bmatrix} \text{RELN} & \text{sand} \\ \text{ROLES} & <[\text{AGT}[1]][\textit{sup}],[\text{TH}[3]]> \\ \text{ADJ–ROLES} & <[\text{REC}[2]]^{[+r]}> \end{bmatrix}
\end{bmatrix}
$$

(187) a.   The board was sanded (for him) (by the carpenter).
      b.   *He was sanded the board.

The failure of *for*-dative inner object recipients to passivize in English is a striking fact, considering that otherwise all non-stative verbs in English do passivize. This includes of course the very verbs which resist passivization when the benefactive is present, as we have just seen. As far as I know, the *only* systematic gap among the passives of ditransitives are these recipients which alternate with *for*-PPs. As we have seen, this gap falls into place automatically on the present analysis.

Certain passives are not quite as bad as this would predict. Many people find sentences like *John was baked a cake* to be acceptable. I think it is plausible that certain common verbs can be lexicalized as 3-place. In particular, with verbs of cooking or preparing food it is perfectly natural to assume that there might be a third argument role for a recipient since food is normally cooked for consumption. Verbs such as *cook* or *bake* might simply be lexicalized as triadic by some speakers, and for them the passivized recipient should be acceptable. Thus sentences like (188a) are fine given the presupposition that John likes his steak burned, as noted by Green 1974; but similar presuppositions cannot save (188b) because *burn* is lexically dyadic:

(188) a. John would like someone to burn him a steak. (see Green 1974)
   b. *John would like to be burned a steak.

Secondly, we predict that the addition of the *for*-dative NP will make the theme NP syntactically obligatory for dyadic or *for*-dative verbs which otherwise allow the theme to be omitted. For example, the theme argument of *cook* is optional (see 189b) but becomes obligatory when the recipient appears (c).

(189) < agt , th > verbs: *cook, knit, crochet, steal, play, sing...*
   a. Mary cooked the children a turkey.
   b. Mary cooked.
   c. *Mary cooked the children.
      'Mary cooked for the children.'

This contrasts with triadic or *to*-dative verbs, which vary from verb to verb regarding the omissibility of the theme NP. With many verbs the theme is optional, as shown in (190).

(190) a. He refused to tell the authorities (the story).
   b. The waitress is serving the customer (a steak).
   c. Shelley fed Leo (some oatmeal).
   d. The customer paid the waitress (the money).
   e. Robert wired/faxed/radioed me (the information).
   f. John showed me (his pit bull).

The behavior of the inner object recipient in forcing the theme to be obligatory is consistent with the behavior of other copredicators (cp. section 1 above). Recall from our discussion of copredication that prepositions have precisely the same effect: often the preposition requires both of its arguments to be syntactically expressed, not just the prepositional object, but another co-argument as well, as in (109) above, repeated as (191a). With NP[*int.rec*], we observe the same phenomenon: it makes the theme syntactically obligatory, as we saw in (189).

(191) a. load the truck with hay
     a'. *load* < agt , (th$_i$) , (loc$_j$) > & *with* < loc$_j$, th$_i$ >

     b. cook the children a turkey
     b'. cook < agt , (th) > & INT.REC < agt, rec, th >

Since the inner object position is restricted to 'intended recipients', this position itself acts as a configurationally encoded copredicator. We can think of the inner object position as a special morpheme, semantically and functionally comparable to a preposition. This configurational copredicator takes the theme as an argument, hence it has the power to require that the theme be syntactically expressed, which in fact it does. This explains why the theme becomes obligatory when the inner object benefactive appears.

In contrast, triadic predicates like *serve* vary regarding the optionality of the theme, as we saw in (190). In such verbs the recipient is an argument of the verb and not an adjunct, and the [+r] feature on the recipient is optional, as needed independently to allow for passivization of the recipient, as in *The customer was served (by the waitress)*. So the recipient is free to link to the unrestricted NP whenever the Theme is not expressed. Thus there is no copredication, and these sentences are just normal transitives.

(192) The waitress is serving the customer.
     serve

$$\left[\begin{array}{l} \text{SUBCAT} < NP_{[1]}, NP_{[2]} > \\ \text{ROLES} < [AGT[1]], [TH[2]] > \end{array}\right]$$

Since the recipient NP is semantically unrestricted there is no copredication and so the theme is not protected from omission. So once again we correctly predict a constrast between inner object arguments (ROLES) versus adjuncts (ADJ.ROLES); moreover our conclusion that the benefactive is an adjunct explains the implicational relation between the presence of the benefactive and the presence of the theme, an otherwise mysterious fact.

A final contrast between *for-* and *to*-datives concerns the presuppositional scope of the prefix *re-* (see Chapter 2, section 2.1 above) in examples like the following:

(193) a.   John re-sent her the book.
           presupposes: the book was previously sent *to her*
       b.   John reheated her some soup.
           presupposes: the soup was previously hot (not necessarily for
           her)

Thus the recipient of *re-send* is in the presuppositional scope of *re-*(as noted in Chapter 2, section 2, fn. 15), while the recipient of *reheat* is not. Let us assume that the semantic contribution by the prefix *re-* to the meaning of its host verb is calculated at the lexical level, i.e., with respect to the lexically specified roles of the host verb. Then it follows that it will take scope over roles but not adjuncts. This suggests that *send* but not *heat* has a recipient role.

Further evidence that the inner object is semantically restricted comes from secondary predication. In English one test for terms (unrestricted complements) is the possibility of controlling depictive predicates (state predicates), as in the following example (from Bresnan 1982:323):

(194) a.   I presented it to John dead.
       b.   *I presented John with it dead.

The AP *dead* can be predicated of the term (*it*) in (194a) but not the oblique (*to John*) in (b). Like PPs, inner object recipients disallow such predication, as seen by the fact that (195a), like (195b), is only two ways and not three ways ambiguous.

(195) a.   John served Mary the salad undressed.
               ⇒ John undressed/ salad undressed/ *?Mary undressed
       b.   John served the salad to Mary undressed.
               ⇒ John undressed/ salad undressed/ *?Mary undressed

In (a) either John or the salad can be interpreted as undressed, but not Mary. Bresnan (1982:323) suggests a constraint against recipients controlling state predicates, but this is not correct:

(196) a.   Mary received the salad undressed.
               ⇒ salad undressed/ Mary undressed
       b.   Mary was served the salad undressed.
               ⇒ salad undressed/ Mary undressed

A recipient linked to the subject NP is perfectly happy to be undressed. Thus the inner objects cleave away from the other (unrestricted) NPs and instead pattern with obliques in disallowing predication. This is consistent with our claim that the inner object, like the obliques, is semantically restricted; indeed our notion of 'semantically restricted' complements is essentially a reconstruction of the traditional category of oblique.

To summarize, we have argued that the inner object recipients in sentences such as *TeX Mary a file*, i.e. roughly those which alternate with *for*-PPs, are with regard to semantics not arguments but adjuncts; however they are linked to complements and so they have most of the syntactic properties of complements: for example, they are sisters of VP. It was proposed that this state of affairs is possible in general with adjuncts as long as they are linked to *restricted* complements such as PPs or semantically restricted NPs. This predicts that the *for*-datives should behave differently from the *to*-datives; this prediction was confirmed by the asymmetry regarding ease of passivization (*to*-datives are easier) and theme-omission (some *to*-datives allow omission of the theme, while no *for*-datives do); and the scope of the prefix *re*- (it takes scope over *to*-dative recipients but not *for*-dative recipients). Finally, we saw further evidence that the inner object is restricted, from the fact that like other restricted complements it resists depictive predication.

5 Comparison with previous analyses

Let us compare our analysis of the *for*-datives with some alternatives. First consider the possibility that verbs like *carve* have an optional benefactive role. As we noted above, this goes contrary to all proposals for determining the valence of a verb as a function of its meaning. Moreover this would treat *carve* exactly like *send*, which begs an explanation for the asymmetries between the two types which have just been shown. Also, since benefactive shift applies to new verbs, this analysis would still require some sort of productive lexicalization rule to ensure that the optional benefactive is included in each new lexical entry.

Next consider zero-affixation analyses. According to M. Baker's 1988 analysis the preposition *for* has a null affixal allomorph which moves onto the verb from its d-structure position, i.e. the position where the preposition would have appeared. But this purported zero affix is difficult to motivate on morphological grounds. For one thing we should expect to find suppletion for this affix, since suppletion is otherwise common in all types of English morphology—but in fact there is not a single instance of it.

Secondly, this analysis runs into trouble with coordination of *to*-dative and *for*-dative verbs as in (197c).

(197) a.   Marie designed a gazebo for them/*to them.
     b.   Marie sold a gazebo to them/(*)for them.
     c.   Marie [designed and sold] them a gazebo.

On the most prominent interpretation of (c) the gazebo is designed *for* and sold *to* the same people (there is a marginal interpretation, which I am ignoring here, in which it is designed for and sold *for* them).[11] The preposition-incorporation analysis puts contradictory demands on the D-structure of (197c), since the NP *them* would have to originate both in a *for*-phrase and in a *to*-phrase. For us this example is not problematical, since the semantics of the inner object NP is compatible with both *to*-dative and *for*-dative verbs.

Aside from the morphological and syntactic difficulties, there is an important distinction which is lost if we try to assimilate the English benefactive shift to morpholexical or 'affix-mediated' (Marantz 1984, Ch. 4) valency-increasing phenomena such as applicatives, preverbs, and genuine preposition incorporation. Unlike the English *for*-datives inner objects, the applied objects often passivize, as in the Swedish preposition incorporation in (198) or applied objects in Chichewa in (199).

---

[11]An analysis in which V' is coordinated ([[designed] and [sold her]] a gazebo) will rescue some examples but it is not always possible:

(i)   a.   The boss gave a company car to her/*for her.
      b.   The boss insured a company car for her/*to her.
      c.   The boss [gave and insured] her a company car.
        (cp. *?The boss gave a company car.)

(ii)   a.   She alternately [prepared and fed] the lions their food.
      b.   They either handed or saved each student her diploma.

With *give, hand,* and *feed* the recipient is obligatory, so the coordinate V' analysis is not possible.

(198) Swedish.

    a. De **tog** chefskapet **från** honom.
        they took the.headship from him

    b. De **fråntog** honom chefskapet.
        they from-took him   the.headship
        'They took the headship from him.'

    c. Han fråntogs   chefskapet.
        he   from-took-PAS the-headship
        'He was deprived of the headship.'

(199) Chichewa (Alsina and Mchombo 1993)

        Mwala u-ku-phwány-**ír**-idw-á   dengu   (ndí anyani).
        3-stone 3s-PR-break-**AP**-PAS-FV 5-basket by 2-baboons
        'The stone is being used (by the baboons) to break the basket.'

(AP = applicative marker) Preposition incorporation and morphological operations like applicative presumably create new verbs with higher valency (by one) than the underived verb; they add not ADJ.ROLES but ROLES. The verb *fråntog* 'deprive' and *tog* 'took' in (198) are simply two different verbs with different valences, so there is no reason to expect *fråntog* to (necessarily) have the special properties we noted for the English *for*-datives, such as difficulty of passivization. Instead we expect it to act like any ditransitive; and we expect this to contrast with English *for*-datives.

    The present analysis is compatible with the proposal in Marantz 1984 to effectively eliminate lexical operations on argument structure altogether. Instead each morpheme (e.g. applicative markers) contributes syntactic or semantic features to a word. For example, the passive affix says in effect 'my highest direct role is suppressed' (see (160) above). From that assumption, it follows that if there is no affixation, as in the English benefactive alternation, then there can be no such affix-encoded features affecting valency; while in the case of applicativization there can be such features.

    In so far as it pertains to predicate valency, we will interpret Marantz's proposal as explaining all non-affix-mediated argument structure alternation in terms of *role optionality* and *optionality of the feature [+r]*. In contrast, role-suppression (passive) and role-addition (applicativization, etc.) must be accompanied by verbal morphology. If this can be maintained, then we predict that the presence of a suppressed role must be signalled by affixation, as in the passive sentences in (200a,b,c,d), while the absence of a role altogether need not be, as in the unaccusative constructions in (200a',b',c',d'). This is shown by well-known contrasts with respect to the possibility of purpose clauses and instrumentals and other contrasts:

(200) a.   The cookies were baked with an oven.
      a'.   The cookies baked (*with an oven).
      b.   The cookies were baked in order to bribe the teacher.
      b'.   The cookies baked (*in order to bribe the teacher).
      c.   These cookies were baked with a friend.
      c'.   The cookies are baking (*with a friend).
      d.   It took 30 minutes for the cookies to be baked.
          (can include time of agent's preparations as well)
      d'.   It took 30 minutes for the cookies to bake.
          (includes only the time in the oven)

That is, the verb *bake* has an optional agent role, while the passive has a suppressed agent role:

(201) a.   bake (active)
        [ROLES < (AG) , TH >]

      b.   baked (passive)
        [ROLES < AG[*sup*] , TH >]

Since *by* only marks suppressed roles, and suppression must be indicated morphologically, it follows that non-affix-mediated middle constructions should not allow *by*-phrases:

(202) This bread cuts easily (*by John).

This is also illustrated by Modern Greek, which has both affixal and non-affixal middles, as shown in (203).

(203) Greek middles (Condoravdi 1989).

    a. Afto to psomi kovete   efkola akoma ki apo pedia.
        this the bread cut-MP3sg easily still and by children
        'This bread can be cut easily even by children.'

    b. * Afti i   porta anigi   akoma ki apo pedia.
        this the door open-3sg still and by children
        'This door opens even by children.'

The affixal middle in (203a) allows a by-phrase but the non-affixal middle in (203b) does not. This supports our hypothesis that valence changes such as suppression must be indicated morphologically.

Turning now to valence-*increasing* processes— that is, processes which add ROLES— the proposal to reduce argument structure alternations to optionality entails that these processes *must* be affix-mediated. This proposal forces us to treat the English benefactive as an adjunct (an ADJ.ROLE). So if this theoretical assumption is correct then it actually predicts the distinctions between benefactive shift in English versus applicativization and true preposition incorporation.

Finally, some analyses have been proposed which are similar to the present one, except with a restriction on the second object instead of the first (Chomsky 1981:171ff). Most assume that it is restricted to a thematic role known as 'Theme'. Chomsky (1981) makes two distinct proposals regarding ditransitives, one of which involved a thematically restricted second object. He suggests that in *John gave Bill a book*, *Bill* receives structural Case from the verb while *a book* receives inherent Case (Chomsky 1981:170), where inherent Case is the GB analogue of thematically restricted linking: 'Structural Case in general is dissociated from θ-role; it is a structural property of a formal configuration. Inherent Case is presumably closely linked to θ-role.' (Chomsky 1981:171). But such analyses do not explain any of the facts set forth above, not even the fact that the roles of the inner object is restricted to recipients, since there is nothing to prevent a ditransitive with an inner object instrumental, privative, or some other role. Also, Smith (1992) has argued on theoretical grounds against restricting complements to the thematic role 'theme'.

6 Restricted NP complements in Swedish and Dutch

In Swedish ditransitives either the theme or the recipient may passivize:

(204) a. Läraren   har   givit   honom boken.
          the-teacher   has   given   him   the-book

     b. Han har givit-s   boken.
          He has give-PAS the.book
          'He has been given the book.'

     c. Boken   har givits   honom.
          the.book has give-PAS him

In Swedish the subject appears in the preverbal position, modulo the verb-second constraint.[12] Either the theme or the recipient can have behavioral subject properties such as the ability to be raised:

(205) a. Han   verkar ha   givit-s   boken.
          he   seems   have give-PAS   the.book
          'He seems to have been given the book.'

     b. Boken   verkar ha   givit-s   honom.
          the.book seems   have give-PAS   him

See Anward 1981 on Swedish and Åfarli 1989a,b on Norwegian, which shares this property with Swedish.

     Swedish resembles English in that the order of nominal complements is fixed:

(206) a. Läraren   har   givit   honom boken.
          the-teacher   has   given   him   the-book
          'The teacher has given him the book.'

     b. *Läraren har givit boken honom.

The facts of Swedish fall out naturally under the same analysis we posited for English, with the sole difference being that the Swedish passive lacks the 'case absorption' effect, i.e. the restricted NP[int.rec] is available in the passive.

---

[12]In all of the Germanic languages discussed here except English the finite verb appears in second position in main clauses. I am following the standard practise of taking subordinate and non-finite clauses as basic and abstracting away from the verb-second phenomenon.

(207) Swedish subcat lists.[13] (X≠N)
       [SUBCAT < NP , (NP[*int.rec*]), (NP), XP* >]

Compare the English subcat list in (152) above. Swedish *giva* has exactly the same argument structure as English *give*.

(208) *giva* 'give'
       [ROLES < AG, REC[±r], TH >]

As in English the [+*r*] feature on the recipient is optional. Since the restricted NP is still available in the Swedish passive (unlike American English), the recipient can remain in post-verbal position in the passive, and so the two options give rise to the two passives.

(209) Han har givits boken. (=(200a))
       givits (passive)
$$\left[\begin{array}{l} \text{SUBCAT} \quad < NP_{[1]}, NP_{[2]} > \\ \text{ROLES} \quad < [AGT][sup], [REC[1]], [TH[2]] > \end{array}\right]$$

---

[13] This subcat list is a simplification in the following sense. Swedish has a relatively unproductive, lexicalized process of preposition incorporation (PI) (see (198) above). The ditransitive 'applied object' form in (198b) has the two passives, just like a basic ditransitive:

(i)   Han   fråntogs   chefskapet.
       he   from-took-PAS the-headship

(ii)   Chefskapet   fråntogs   honom.
       the-headship   from-took-PAS him
       'He was deprived of the headship.'

Further examples: *avlocka* lit. 'from-elicit' (*De avlockade Johan en bekännelse* 'They drew a confession from John.'); *påtvinga* lit. 'on-force' (*påtvinga honom något* 'force something on him'). The existence of these verbs means that only in non-PI verbs is the inner object restricted to recipients. In PI verbs the inner object takes whatever thematic role is licensed by the prefixed preposition. One approach to this phenomenon within the present framework would be to posit a general rule creating restricted complements from prepositional prefixes: $P_\theta \Rightarrow NP[\theta]$ (although as noted this process is not fully productive.) Like recipients, the role added through PI is [±r]: *fråntaga* < agt , source([±r]) , th >. This would allow for the two passives in (ii). See Ejerhed 1983 and Åkermalm 1961 for further discussion.

(210) Boken har givits honom. (=(200b))
givits (passive)

$$\begin{bmatrix} \text{SUBCAT} & < \text{NP}_{[2]}, \text{NP}[\textit{int. rec}]_{[1]} > \\ \text{ROLES} & < [\text{AGT}][\textit{sup}], [\text{REC}[1]]^{[+r]}, [\text{TH}[2]] > \end{bmatrix}$$

Clear evidence that the NP[*REC*] complement is available for passives as well as actives is that in impersonal passives of ditransitives both objects remain inside the VP (Åfarli 1989a,b):

(211) Det har givits   honom en bok.
      it   has give.PAS him   a   book
      'He has been given a book.'

The subject of (211) is the expletive (expl) *det*, and the other complements link up just as they would in an active, with the theme following the recipient.

(212) *givits (expletive)*

$$\begin{bmatrix} \text{SUBCAT} & < \text{NP}_{[expl]}, \text{NP}[\textit{int. rec}]_{[1]}, \text{NP}_{[2]} > \\ \text{ROLES} & < [\text{AGT}][\textit{sup}], [\text{REC}[1]]^{[+r]}, [\text{TH}[2]] > \end{bmatrix}$$

Evidence for the semantically restricted NP[*int.rec*] can be found in Swedish adjective phrases, where bare NPs may occur only if they have the role of recipient:[14]

(213) a. den   [generalen   givna]$_{AP}$ medaljen
          the   the-general   given   medal
          'the medal (which was) given to the general'

    b. *den [medaljen   givna]$_{AP}$ generalen
          the   the-medal   given   general
          'the general (who was) given the medal'

---

[14]This was pointed out to me by Paul Kiparsky.

(214) a. Det är   [mig likgiltigt]_{AP}.
        it is   me   indifferent)
        'It's all the same to me.'

      b. *Gatan   är [bilar tom]_{AP}
        the.street i s cars empty
        'The street is empty of cars.'

This is reminiscent of the pattern found with (morphological) datives in German (from Cole et al 1980:728):

(215) a. Das vom Jungen gelesene   Buch heisst 'Sieben Legenden'.
        the by.the boy read   book is.called seven legends
        'The book read by the boy is called "Seven Legends."'

      b. *Der vom   Lehrer geholfene Junge bekam eine gute Note.
        the by.the teacher helped boy got   a   good grade.
        ('The boy helped by the teacher got a good grade.')

In other words, the Swedish recipients preserve some of the properties of oblique case marking, although Swedish lacks case.

     Indeed, while in contemporary Swedish ditransitives allow both passives shown in (204), it is worth noting that as recently as the turn of the century Swedish conformed to the German/Dutch pattern, where only the theme passivizes. Passivizing the 'semantic dative' (the recipient role) was an innovation, as reflected even in relatively recent Swedish usage manuals, as in the following (Wellander 1973:148; translation follows):

När dylika verb brukas passivt är det enligt gammal grammatisk regel ackusativobjektet som blir subjekt: *Ett äpple gavs honom av modern,* icke dativobjektet: *Han gavs ett äpple av modern.* Då substantivet i vårt språk har samma form för dativ och ackusativ är emellertid känslan för skillnaden mellan dessa kasus hos många föga klar. Därmed är grunden för den grammatiska regeln i stor utsträckning raserad; nutidens svenskar, av vilka många studerat engelska men få tyska och än färre latin, saknar den omedelbara känsla för kasusskillnaden som gör regeln lätt att iaktta.

When such verbs are used in the passive, according to an old grammatical rule the accusative object becomes the subject: *An apple was given him by mother,* not the dative object: *He was given an apple by mother.* However, since nominals in our language have the same form for dative and accusative, for many speakers a feeling for the distinction between these cases is unclear. Consequently the basis for the grammatical rule is to a large extent obliterated; contemporary Swedes, of whom many study English but few German and even fewer Latin, lack the immediate feeling for case distinctions which make the rule easy to follow. [S.W.]

Given that recipient-passivization came in long after dative case morphology was lost, what Wellander characterizes as losing a feeling for the dative *case* is perhaps more accurately described as (optionally) losing the feature [+r].

Like Swedish, Dutch lacks case inflection on full NPs, and even in pronouns there is no accusative-dative distinction, but in contrast with Swedish the Dutch recipients are obligatorily [+r].

First consider word order in Dutch. In monotransitive nominative-accusative clauses the nominative must precede the accusative.[15]

(216) a. ...dat de jongen de boeken heeft gelezen.
   ...that the boy(sg) the books(pl) has(sg) read
   'that the boy has read the books.'

  b. ?*...de boeken de jongen heeft gelezen.

Likewise, in active ditransitives the linear order of nominal complements cannot deviate from the order Agent < Recipient < Theme:

(217) a. ...dat Jan de kinderen de boeken heeft gegeven.
   ...that John the children the books has given
   'that John has given the children the books.'

  b. *...Jan de boeken de kinderen heeft gegeven.

While in the active form in (217) above the recipient must precede the theme, the order is freer in passives. A passivized theme either follow or precede the recipient:

(218) a. ...dat Marie de boeken werden gegeven.
   ...that Marie the books were-pl given
   'that Marie was given the books.'
  b. ...dat de boeken Marie werden gegeven.

---

[15]Unless indicated otherwise, the Dutch data is due to Annie Zaenen, whom I wish to thank.

(218a) with the recipient preceding the theme is the more natural order, according to den Besten (1985), but both are perfectly grammatical. While Dutch lacks case marking on full NPs, notice that the Theme *de boeken* 'the books' triggers agreement, a point to which we return below.[16]

Dutch psychological verbs such as *bevallen* 'like' parallel the passive *gegeven* rather than actives like *lezen* 'read' ((216) above) in allowing both orders (den Besten 1985, Zaenen 1987):

(219) ...dat   Jan   de   boeken zijn   bevallen.
       ...that   John   the   books   AUX   pleased
       'that the books have pleased John.'

(220) ...dat   de boeken   Jan   zijn   bevallen.
       ...that   the books   John   AUX   pleased
       'that the books have pleased John.'

To sum up, Dutch has fixed NP complement order in actives, but relatively free order in passives of ditransitives. The theme and not the recipient has subject properties in passivized ditransitives.

These facts are neatly explained if we assume that Dutch has a subcategorization list very similar to that of English and Swedish. The restriction on the second NP is either to recipients (as in English and Swedish) or to experiencers, the two semantic restrictions associated with German dative case.

(221) Dutch subcat list. (X≠N)
       [SUBCAT < (NP), (NP{[*rec*]/[*exp*]}), (NP), XP* >]

The sole difference in argument structure of ditransitives like *give* is that in Dutch the [+r] feature is obligatory, while it is optional in Swedish and English:

(222) *geven*   'give'
       [ROLES   < [AGT], [REC][+r], [TH] >]

Take actives first. As shown in above, active sentences with two unrestricted roles have strict word order. This follows from the Isomorphy Condition.

---

[16]Some Dutch speakers allow the recipient to trigger agreement, especially in main clauses.

(223) *lezen*   'read'
$$\begin{bmatrix} \text{SUBCAT} & < NP_{[1]}, NP_{[2]} > \\ \text{ROLES} & < [AGT[1]], [TH[2]] > \end{bmatrix}$$

The same applies to active ditransitives, which also have two unrestricted roles. There is only one way to link the roles of a verb like 'give'.

(224) *geven*   'give'
$$\begin{bmatrix} \text{SUBCAT} < NP_{[1]}, NP[rec]_{[2]}, NP_{[3]} > \\ \text{ROLES} < [AGT[1]], [REC[2]]^{[+r]}, [TH[3]] > \end{bmatrix}$$

Since the recipient is [+r], the only NP it can link to is NP[rec]. The other two NPs are unrestricted, so the lines of association cannot cross (by the Isomorphy Condition). Since linear order of sisters is determined by obliqueness on the subcat list, and the VP is verb-final, the surface order mirrors the subcat list order no matter what ID structure we assume.

But in a verb with two roles, one restricted and one unrestricted, there are two possible linkings, since the unrestricted role has two options. In passives of ditransitives the recipient must link to NP[rec], and the theme links either to the NP on its left or the NP on its right.

(225) ...dat Marie de boeken werden gegeven.
gegeven 'given'
$$\begin{bmatrix} \text{SUBCAT} < NP[rec]_{[2]}, NP_{[3]} > \\ \text{ROLES} < [AGT][sup], [REC[2]]^{[+r]}, [TH[3]] > \end{bmatrix}$$

(226) ...dat de boeken Marie werden gegeven.
gegeven 'given'
$$\begin{bmatrix} \text{SUBCAT} < NP_{[3]}, NP[rec]_{[2]} > \\ \text{ROLES} < [AGT][sup], [REC[2]]^{[+r]}, [TH[3]] > \end{bmatrix}$$

This accounts for the two word orders in the passive. The two orderings of the experiencer verbs are derived in the same manner:

(227) *bevallen* 'please'
$$\begin{bmatrix} \text{SUBCAT} < NP_{[2]}, NP[exp]_{[1]} > \\ \text{ROLES} < [EXP[1]]^{[+r]}, [TH[2]] > \end{bmatrix}$$

(228) *bevallen* 'please'

$$\begin{bmatrix} \text{SUBCAT} < \text{NP}[exp]_{[1]}, \text{NP}_{[2]} > \\ \text{ROLES} < [\text{EXP}[1]]^{[+r]}, [\text{TH}[2]] > \end{bmatrix}$$

Just as in the passives of ditransitives which we saw in (218) above, the active experiencer verbs have one restricted (experiencer) role linked to a restricted NP; since the Isomorphy Condition only applies to unrestricted roles, lines of association may cross and so both orders are allowed.

Now consider subjecthood. I will assume that universally subject complements cannot be [+r] (Bresnan and Kanerva 1989). Instead the subject is defined as the highest unrestricted complement (Kiparsky 1987; Smith 1992).[17]

Since the experiencers and recipients are [+r] we predict that these complements will lack subject properties. This prediction is correct. First of all, recall that the theme NP and not the recipient triggers plural agreement in passive. Also, when pronominal it is the theme and not the recipient which appears in nominative.

(229) a.   ...hij   haar   de boeken heeft   gegeven.
          ...he.nom.sg her.non-nom   the books has.sg given
          'he has given her the books'

      b.   ...zij   haar   werden gegeven.
          ...they.nom.pl her.non-nom were.pl given
          'they were given (to) her.'

      c.   *...hij   de boeken werd   gegeven.
          ...he.nom the books was.sg given
          ('he was given the books.')

In addition, the recipient cannot be controlled (230a), in contrast to unrestricted roles (230b).

---

[17]See Chapter 4, section 3 below for a more adequate account of subjecthood.

(230) from den Besten 1985

    a.   *Hij hoopt dat boek toegestuurd te worden.
        he hopes that book sent   to be
        ('He hopes to be sent that book.')

    b.   Hij hoopt niet ontslagen te zullen worden.
        he hopes not fired   to will be
        'He hopes not to be fired.'

Similar facts apply to the experiencer verbs. Only the theme and not the experiencer can be controlled, so that control constructions like (231) are unambiguous.

(231) a.   Jan hoopt Marie te bevallen.
        Jan hopes Marie to please.inf
        'John hopes to please Mary.'
        (not: 'John hopes that Mary will please him.'

    b.   Hem bevallen is niet moeilijk.
        him please.inf is not difficult
        'To please him is not difficult.'
        (not: 'To be pleased by him is not difficult.')

These sentences lack the interpretation in which the experiencer is controlled, thus adding further support to the claim that the experiencer cannot be the subject. This follows immediately if the experiencer is [+r].

In conclusion, we have seen evidence that Swedish and Dutch, like English, has an NP object option which is restricted to the recipient role; and in Dutch this NP has an alternative restriction to the experiencer role. Regarding ditransitives we identified two parameters of variation: first, whether the [+r] classification on the recipient role is optional (English, Swedish) or obligatory (Dutch); and second, whether the restricted NP[REC] is available in the passive (Swedish, Dutch) or not (English). (In addition, Dutch VPs are verb-final while English and Swedish are verb-initial.)

(232) Parameters of variation.

	recipient role	'case absorption'
English	[±r]	yes
Swedish	[±r]	no
Dutch	[+r]	no

With these two simple parameters we have accounted for a seemingly diverse set of facts, including word order linking in the passive.

7 Overview of the theory

In this chapter we expanded our theory to cover obliques and investigated their special role in linking. We argued that the English dative alternation is best explained without any rule whatsoever, at any level of structure: instead, we hypothesize that English has a restricted NP complement, and that recipient roles therefore have two options for linking, the restricted NP or the *to*-PP. This also provided an account of *for*-dative type recipients, which have the paradoxical property of being semantically adjunct-like but syntactically complement-like. To explain this we suggested that these roles are in fact semantic adjuncts realized as complements, a state of affairs which, we suggested, is possible only with semantically restricted complements.

Let us step back and consider the broader questions our theory has addressed. How large a role does lexicosemantic content play in syntax? How precise or vague a role does it play? One reason why these questions have been difficult for linguists to answer is that our tools for analyzing word meaning for this particular purpose have been too blunt to make clear and testable hypotheses. In this work I have tried to remedy this problem in two ways, first by providing some sharper tools; and second by carefully choosing the proper places to make the cuts, so as not to place unnecessary demands on the lexical semantic theory.

Taking the latter point first, I have assumed that the connection between the semantic content of a verb and its argument structure is quite direct. It is not mediated by first classifying all the roles into thematic role types, then stating argument structure rules on those classifications. Nor is it mediated by a level of lexical conceptual structure. As a result it is not necessary, on the present assumptions, to regiment every argument role into a uniform 'level of representation' by embedding the roles in a set of thematic role types or positions in lexical conceptual structure.

Instead, the restricted roles need not be assigned to a universal type, but are linked according to whatever parochial semantic relations happen to be expressible by the adpositions, case markers, and so on, of a given language. While this set of relations (recipient, instrument, benefactive, etc.) is broadly similar across languages, the specific semantic contours of corresponding adpositions are notoriously variable across languages, at least in matters of detail. While the same preposition selection *rule* applies across languages, the result of applying the rule depends on the meanings of the prepositions to which it applies.

By not assuming that every role of every verb falls into one or another universal category, we avoid one of the more vexing problems of traditional thematic role type theories, the difficulty or impossibility of identifying them with any confidence, except in the simplest cases— a problem which was discussed at length in Chapter 1 above. From the point of view of acquisition, unless this problem can be solved it would seem to cast doubt on the thematic roles enterprise since children acquiring language would have to have access to classification schemes considerably more precise than anything linguists have been capable of specifying. Instead of assuming a universal set of thematic role types, we have associated semantic relations (*INT.REC, INT.CAUSE.REC, EXP*, etc.) with specific forms such as the prepositions *to* and *for* and the restricted NP complements. The semantics of these relations is assimilable to the more general problem of lexical semantics of prepositions and other forms. The acquisition of lexical meaning, like the problem of lexical semantics generally, is a problem that is far from solved. But we do know that children in fact learn the meanings of prepositions. In other words, the child does not need to learn to apply a thematic role classification schema on top of her task of learning word and morpheme meanings.

In contrast, the unrestricted roles are treated to a universal semantic classification, but it is a classification which is subject to extra-linguistic verification. This extra-linguistic verification involves only a bare minimum amount of conceptual structure. Recall the Notion-Rule (51), repeated here.

(233) The Notion-Rule.

A lexical sign meeting this description is ill-formed:

$$* \begin{bmatrix} \text{REL} & R \\ \text{ROLES} & <\ldots[\text{ROLE1}]\ldots[\text{ROLE2}]\ldots> \end{bmatrix},$$

if the following lexical entailment holds:
$$\forall x, y \, \Box [R \, (\text{ROLE1}:y, \text{ROLE2}:x) \rightarrow CONCEIVE(x,y)]$$

We know that the verb *like* fits the structural description of this rule because for x to like y means x has a notion of (*CONCEIVEs*) y. To make this determination we are not forced to rely exclusively on our estimate of how speakers of English 'conceptualize' the relation of liking and accordingly posit a 'lexical conceptual structure' on the basis of our estimate. Instead we look at the relation between our minds and the world. It is a fact of the world, as seen through our eyes, that the *real* relation of liking (as that relation is individuated by anyone who understands what the verb *like* means) involves the *real* relation of conceiving (as that relation is individuated by all humans— or so we claim). This puts our extra-linguistic verification on rather firm ground. It also forces us to be explicit about what concepts we assume to be universal. For the purpose of the Notion-Rule it must be assumed that all people are innately endowed with a concept of the *CONCEIVE* relation (or endowed with the potential for developing that concept), the relation which holds between a thing in the world and a cognitive agent entertaining a mental notion of that thing. Arguably the knowledge of this fundamental relation is in frequent use by all of us during our waking hours.

To recapitulate, we have proposed that the problem of linking be broken down into three parts:

(234) [SUBCAT   < ... ... >]   *principles of subcat structure*
                  ⇑ ⇑

                  linking   *principles of linking*
                  ⇓ ⇓

       [ROLES   < ... ... >]   *principles of argument structure*

The principles of subcat structure order the subcat list on the basis of categorial information about the complements (e.g. PPs are more oblique than NPs); we have not dealt with these principles in any detail here. We have proposed two *principles of linking:* the Restricted Linking Principle ((136) above) which states that a restricted role must link to a semantically restricted complement (an 'oblique') whose semantic restriction is appropriate to the role in question; and the Isomorphy Condition ((9) above) which states that the lines of association for unrestricted linking cannot cross. And we have proposed three rules governing argument structure, the first of which we formulated with somewhat greater precision than the other two: the Notion-Rule ((51) above), which involves the semantic relation between an individual and a cognitive agent with a mental conception of that individual; the Nuclear Role Rule ((79) above), which deals with the aspectual or temporal structure of events; and the Part Rule ((98) above), which involves the basic part relation holding between quantities of matter.

The following chapter, which was written several years after chapters 1-3, presents some ideas for reformulating these proposals within a hierarchical lexicon.

4

Reformulations in the Hierarchical Lexicon

The preceding chapters were written three years ago. As I look back at the proposals contained in them, it becomes apparent that some of them can be improved with a few changes in their formulation. First of all, recall the semantic side of our argument selection rules (the Notion-Rule, etc.) and the rule for preposition selection (the Restricted Linking Priniciple). Each of these involves positing a lexical entailment. For example, the argument selection rules work by stating that whenever a certain entailment obtains, then a particular ordering of arguments is disallowed. The alternative to be explored below woks by sorting psoa descriptions and stating our rules in terms of subsumption relations between those sorts. We will apply this idea to the Restricted Linking Principle first (section 1), then turn to argument selection rules (section 2). Lastly, in section 3 we will see that the proposal to split off the subject from other complements (Borsley 1987) allows us to capture the way language-wide morphological or categorial constraints on subjects can influence the mapping between argument structure and complement structure. For the purpose of this chapter I will assume some familiarity with the version of HPSG presented in Pollard and Sag 1994.

1 Preposition selection revisited

1.1 Semantically motivated preposition selection

Chapter 3 proposes the Restricted Linking Principle ((136) above), which is responsible for semantically motivated selection of prepositions (as well as postpositions and semantic case). That principle states, in effect, that if an appropriate relation holds between the semantic content of a verb V and the content of a preposition P, then V may select P to head a complement PP. It would clearly be preferable if the effects of the RLP could be acheived without recourse to this stipulation. An alternative view which avoids this stipulative character and seems preferable on empirical grounds is proposed in Wechsler 1994, building on proposals by Tony Davis (1993, forthcoming).[1]

---

[1] See also the brief suggestion in Pollard and Sag 1994:342-343.

To take a simple example, consider the selection of a PP[*to*] and a PP[*about*] by many communicative act verbs like *talk, sing, murmur,* and so on:

(235) John talked (to Mary) (about Bill).

(236) John ate (*to Mary) (*about Bill).

The basis of our approach to explaining preposition selection is very straightforward. We assign appropriate semantic content to the various prepositions and other elements. General rules of compositional semantics build up the meaning of the VP from the meanings of V and its complement PPs. Once this is done, it is no longer necessary for verbs to select prepositions explicitly. The improper selections are ruled out on pragmatic grounds, because the resulting semantic combinations do not make sense. Thus (235) is acceptable because the meanings of *talk, to,* and *about* are compatible in the proper way, while (236) is ruled out because the meanings of *eat* and *to* and the meanings of *eat* and *about* are incompatible.

To see how this works, let (237) be the lexical sign for (one-place) *talk.* Its content is a psoa with only one participant, namely the talker.

(237)

$$
\begin{bmatrix}
\text{PHON} & <\text{talk}> \\
\text{SUBCAT} & <\text{NP}_{[1]}> \\
\text{CONTENT} & \begin{bmatrix} communicative\text{-}act\text{-}psoa \\ \text{REL} & talk \\ \text{SOURCE} & [1] \end{bmatrix}
\end{bmatrix}
$$

This lexical sign specifies that the subject of *talk* is an NP whose INDEX is token-identical to the filler of the talker (SOURCE) role. Note that I have departed from the ordered roles approach in the previous chapters and instead adopted the more standard view that roles are unordered within the psoa. The ordering will be reintroduced in a different way below (see section 2).

What about the content of a PP like *to Mary* in (235)? As in Chapter 3 above, I posit that a PP, like a verb, denotes a psoa. One difference, though, is that I will suggest that unlike verbs, certain complement prepositions are unspecified for the particular RELATION within their psoas. Instead that relation comes from the verb.

We will posit that every verb in the language automatically inherits a list of zero or more PP complements, which are appended to the end of the verb's SUBCAT list; and that the semantic CONTENT of each PP is unified with that of the verb. (237) above is the lexical sign for *talk* showing only lexically idiosyncratic information; (238) is the lexical sign for the verb *talk* including the zero or more PPs which it has automatically inherited by virtue of being a verb.

(238)

$$
\begin{bmatrix}
\text{PHON} & < \text{talk} > \\
\text{SUBCAT} & < \text{NP}_{[1]}, \text{PP:}[2]^* > \\
\text{CONTENT} & [2] \begin{bmatrix} \textit{communicative--act--psoa} \\ \text{REL} \quad \textit{talk} \\ \text{SOURCE} \quad [1] \end{bmatrix}
\end{bmatrix}
$$

This lexical entry specifies that the CONTENT of *talk* is a psoa with at least one argument (the SOURCE or talker participant), unified with the CONTENTs of any complement PPs. The lexicon allows any PP complement for any verb, but the bad cases are ruled out by world knowledge.

Since all the action is in this world knowledge, we need to say a lot more about how to represent it. In HPSG all feature structures are *sorted*; the sort name appears in italics at the top of the feature structure; e.g. the value of CONTENT in (238) is a feature structure of sort *communicative-act-psoa*. These sorts are organized in a hierarchy of sorts and subsorts: e.g. *communicative-act-psoa* is a subsort of *psoa*.

Let us assume that the RELATION in a psoa does not determine its valency: a psoa with the *talk* relation can be one-place, two-place, three-place, and so on.[2] However, while the relations are not sorted according to valency, I will assume that the psoas are. For example, the psoa subsort called *communicative-act-psoa* includes all communicative act psoas with at least one participant, namely a source participant simply *talking, singing, murmuring* etc.; additionally it may have other participants such as a goal or informational topic. A *monadic-comm-act-psoa* has exactly one participant, namely a source. The *communicate-to-psoa* sort includes psoas like talking-to, singing-to, murmuring-to, etc. with at least a source and a goal; a *dyadic-comm-to-psoa* has source and goal and nothing else. The *communicate-*

---

[2]Variable polyadicity of relations is not always assumed in situation semantics, but I believe it is the best way to capture our intuitions about real situations.

about-psoa sort includes psoas like talking-about, singing-about, murmuring-about, etc.; a *dyadic-comm-about-psoa* has source and theme and nothing else. And the *communicate-to-about-psoa* sort includes triadic psoas like talking-to-X-about-Y, explaining-to-X-about-Y, and so on.

These subsorts are organized in the following inheritance or subsumption hierarchy:

(239)

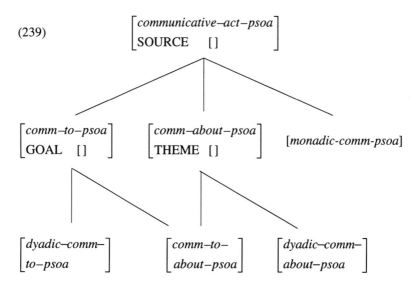

Each feature structure in the hierarchy inherits all the information which dominates it in the lattice. Thus every *communicate-to-psoa* is also a *communicative-act-psoa*, so it has any properties of the supersort.

Note that the lexical signs for *talk* in (237) and (238) indicate that its CONTENT is a psoa of sort *communicative-act-psoa*. The lexical signs below indicate that *about* and *to* denote psoas of sort *commun(icate)-about-psoa* and *communicate-to-psoa* respectively.

(240)

$$\begin{bmatrix} \text{PHON} & <\text{about}> \\ \text{SUBCAT} & <\text{NP}_{[1]}> \\ \text{CONTENT} & \begin{bmatrix} commun-about-psoa \\ \text{THEME} \; [1] \end{bmatrix} \end{bmatrix}$$

(241)

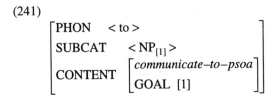

It is part of our world knowledge, as represented by the subsumption lattice in (239), that any combination of these psoa types — *comm-act-psoa*, *comm-about-psoa*, and *comm-to-psoa* — can be unified. It follows that any verb denoting a *comm-act-psoa*, such as *talk*, *sing*, or *murmur*, can combine with a PP[*to*] or a PP[*about*] or both.

By way of illustration, the sign for the sentence *John talked to Mary* is given below:

(242)

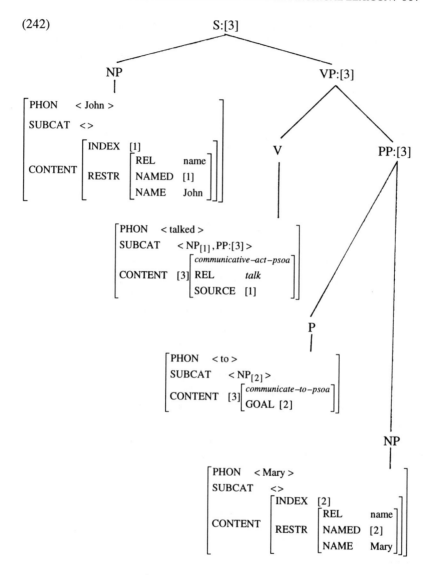

Consider the CONTENT value of the sentence S, that is, the feature structure with the tag [3]. By the Semantics Principle the features [RELATION *talk*] and [SOURCE [1]] are passed up from the verb *talk*. Similarly, the preposition *to* passes the feature [GOAL [2]] up to the content of the PP. The lexical sign for the verb specifies that the contents of its PP complement and the content of the verb itself are structure-shared, so all features of the PP content are shared by the verb content, hence by the sentence content. In diagram (242) I have omitted the GOAL feature from the sign for the verb in order to show more clearly the lexical sources of the various pieces of information.

Collecting the relevant information for sentence sign, we get the following SUBCAT and CONTENT features:[3]

(243)

$$
\begin{bmatrix}
\text{SUBCAT} & <> \\
\text{CONTENT} & [3] \begin{bmatrix} comm-to\text{–}psoa \\ \text{REL} \quad talk \\ \text{SOURCE} \quad [1] \\ \text{GOAL} \quad [2] \end{bmatrix}
\end{bmatrix}
$$

This two-place psoa is the desired result. Notice that we have unified the content values of the verb and the preposition. The features REL, SOURCE, and GOAL are simply 'pooled', as explained above; and since the sort *comm-act-psoa* subsumes *comm-to-psoa*, the unification of the two is the more specific *comm-to-psoa* (i.e. the subsort). Thus a verb will reject a PP complement if that unification fails. For example **John ate to Mary* is ruled out because the sort of *eat*'s CONTENT, whatever it may be (*ingest-psoa* perhaps), will not unify with *comm-to-psoa*.

While *sing* and *talk* are minimally monadic predicates but can optionally have other arguments as well, other verbs of communication like *complain, explain,* and *signal* seem to be semantically three-place: they semantically select for the GOAL and THEME of communication, regardless of whether the PP[*to*] or PP[*about*] appears in the syntax. Thus we must distinguish two types of verbs:

---

[3]From the sort hierarchy in (239) we see that *comm-to-psoa* could be replaced by a more informative sort, namely *dyadic-comm-to-psoa*. Since the sort *comm-to-psoa* is not maximal, the above feature structure is not fully sort-resolved; the corresponding sort-resolved feature structure would be the following:

$$
\begin{bmatrix}
\text{SUBCAT} & <> \\
\text{CONTENT} & [3] \begin{bmatrix} dyadic\text{–}comm-to\text{–}psoa \\ \text{REL} \quad talk \\ \text{SOURCE} \quad [1] \\ \text{GOAL} \quad [2] \end{bmatrix}
\end{bmatrix}
$$

(244) Semantically obligatory PP arguments (*complain, explain, signal, ...*)
    a.   John complained (to Mary) (about the heat).
    b.   John complained. $\models \exists$ x,y |John complained to x about y.

(245) Semantically optional PP arguments (*sing, whistle, talk, ...*)
    a.   John sang (to Mary) (about his homeland).
    b.   John sang. $\not\models \exists$ x | John sang to x.
                            $\not\models \exists$ y | John sang about y.

We capture this valency distinction by specifying that the triadic verbs have a content of sort *commun-to-about-psoa*.

(246)

$$
\begin{bmatrix}
\text{PHON} & <\text{complain}> \\
\text{SUBCAT} & <\text{NP}_{[1]}> \\
\text{CONTENT} & \begin{bmatrix} commun\text{-}to\text{-}about\text{-}psoa \\ \text{REL} \quad\quad complain \\ \text{SOURCE} \quad [1] \end{bmatrix}
\end{bmatrix}
$$

Being of sort *commun-to-about-psoa*, the content of *complain* automatically inherits the GOAL and THEME roles (see (239) above). If a PP[*to*] or PP[*about*] appear in the sentence then they will fill the GOAL and THEME roles, respectively.

A more complete account of preposition selection must (i) prohibit one-to-many mappings from arguments to complements to rule out **John sold me his car to me* (see below on dative shift), **John talked to me to me*, and so on (cp. GB's θ-criterion and LFG's Function-Argument Biuniqueness); and (ii) provide for the interpretation of unprojected arguments (roughly, this involves existential quantification; see (244) and (245) above). The precise formulation of the needed principles will be left for future work.

Like the theory in Chapter 3 above, this analysis gives semantic content to each non-predicative preposition and thereby provides a theory of fine-grained thematic role types. The attribute names like GOAL and THEME are only labels for the argument slots within the psoa in which they occur, so they are formalizations of thematic role types in the sense that they label fine-grained equivalence classes across whatever verbs or prepositions happen to have contents in which the role names occur. For example, certain verbs including *talk* can take an optional GOAL and the preposition *to* marks a GOAL. No further independent theory is assumed or needed to cash out the semantics of GOALs.

1.2 The Dative Alternation Revisited

The proposal in the previous section applies straightforwardly to explain some but not all aspects of the dative alternation that are discussed in Chapter 3 above. As we will see, it allows us to reduce certain transitivity alternations to the syntactic optionality of an NP complement. Consider the alternation observed in the verb *sell:*

(247) a.   John sold me his car.
      b.   John sold his car to me.

We need only posit that one NP of a ditransitive verb like *sell* is syntactically optional.

(248)

$$
\begin{bmatrix}
\text{PHON} & <\text{sell}> \\
\text{SUBCAT} & <\text{NP}_{[1]}\,(\text{NP}_{[2]},)\,\text{NP}_{[3]}> \\
\text{CONTENT} &
\begin{bmatrix}
\textit{transfer–psoa} \\
\text{REL} \quad \textit{sell} \\
\text{SOURCE} \quad [1] \\
\text{GOAL} \quad [2] \\
\text{THEME} \quad [3]
\end{bmatrix}
\end{bmatrix}
$$

The GOAL argument is semantically obligatory (there is no selling without a buyer). When we select the option without the optional NP, a PP[*to*] may automatically be selected to express the GOAL argument, by the mechanism explained in the previous section. Like all verbs, *sell* inherits any number of PP complements (and pragmatics picks out the right ones); suppose it inherits one PP complement:

(249)

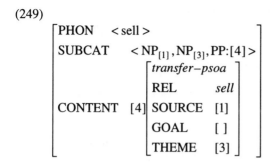

$$
\begin{bmatrix}
\text{PHON} & <\text{sell}> \\
\text{SUBCAT} & <\text{NP}_{[1]}, \text{NP}_{[3]}, \text{PP:}[4]> \\
\text{CONTENT} & [4] \begin{bmatrix} \textit{transfer--psoa} \\ \text{REL} \quad \textit{sell} \\ \text{SOURCE} \quad [1] \\ \text{GOAL} \quad [\ ] \\ \text{THEME} \quad [3] \end{bmatrix}
\end{bmatrix}
$$

Given the following lexical sign for the preposition *to* for transfer of possession—

(250)

$$
\begin{bmatrix}
\text{PHON} & <\text{to}> \\
\text{SUBCAT} & <\text{NP}_{[1]}> \\
\text{CONTENT} & \begin{bmatrix} \textit{transfer--psoa} \\ \text{GOAL} \quad [1] \end{bmatrix}
\end{bmatrix}
$$

—then its content can unify with the content of *sell*, hence a PP headed by this preposition can serve as a complement to *sell*.

More generally, we predict the existence of such alternations from the following basic observation:

(251) Some complements are syntactically optional.

Given this assumption, we would need a special stipulation to explain the *absence* of dative shift. Alternations of this kind are predicted to occur as long as semantically appropriate prepositions are available in the lexicon.

However, this new account does not explain the semantic restrictions on the English ditransitive (NP-NP) construction. In particular, it fails to explain the fact, discussed in Chapter 3 above, that there are no ditransitives with roles other than recipient for the inner object (see (150), repeated here):

(252) *John chopped the ax the tree.

This was explained above by positing a semantically restricted configurational position: the inner object position is restricted to recipients. The restricted position also accounted for the possibility of productively adding the benefactive adjunct (see Chapter 3, section 3). The adaptation of the revised account to address these issues will be left for future research.[4]

1.3 Idiosyncratically selected prepositions

Some preposition selection is essentially idiosyncratic, as shown by comparing semantically similar verbs like *charge* vs. *blame* vs. *accuse: charge Fred* WITH *the crime, blame Fred* FOR *the crime, accuse Fred* OF *the crime.* Such verbs select their prepositions via simple lexical specifications within their complement selection features:

(253) a. *charge*: SUBCAT < NP, NP, PP[*with*] >
 b. *blame*: SUBCAT < NP, NP, PP[*for*] >
 c. *accuse*: SUBCAT < NP, NP, PP[*of*] >

The above proposal for preposition selection predicts different semantic properties for idiosyncratically versus semantically selected PPs. To see why, note first of all that according to our theory, contentful prepositions make possible one type of *argument addition*. (Other types are applicativization, causativization, etc.) Recall that all of the 'added' (i.e. semantically optional) complement PP's lie outside the idiosyncratic lexical domain of the verb. For example, the minimal lexical sign for *talk* is just (3), repeated here:

(254)

$$\begin{bmatrix} \text{PHON} & < \text{talk} > \\ \text{SUBCAT} & < \text{NP}_{[1]} > \\ \text{CONTENT} & \begin{bmatrix} communicative\text{--}act\text{--}psoa \\ \text{REL} & talk \\ \text{SOURCE} & [1] \end{bmatrix} \end{bmatrix}$$

Now recall that all of the added arguments (GOAL, THEME, etc.) are semantically optional. Suppose we further assume that *only* the added arguments are semantically optional. Then we make the following prediction:[5]

---

[4]See Davis forthcoming for some relevant proposals.

[5]The result in (255) is similar in spirit to the part of the GB Projection Principle that states that a lexical item cannot c-select a position unless it θ-marks the phrase filling that position. (cp. Chomsky 1981:38ff: if α subcategorizes the position β, then α θ-marks β.) Note two

(255) Prediction: PP complements with idiosyncratically selected head P's must be semantically obligatory.

To see why this follows, note that the minimal lexical entry for *talk* given in (237) specifies no complement PPs at all so clearly it cannot idiosyncratically select them. Instead, wildcard PPs are inherited by *talk* (see (238)), and by all other verbs. But specific PPs are selected subject only to general semantic and pragmatic constraints which do not mention particular verbs.

As an example of this prediction, the roles expressed by the idiosyncratic PPs of *charge, blame*, and *accuse* (see (253) above), are correctly predicted to be semantically obligatory.

(256) a. They charged John.
$\models \exists$ x I they charged John with x
  b. They blamed John.
$\models \exists$ x I they blamed John for x
  c. They accused John.
$\models \exists$ x I they accused John of x

We predict that we will not find idiosyncratically selected PPs expressing semantically optional argument. For instance we should not find a verb *to zing* which is like *sing* in having a semantically optional goal, but which expresses its theme idiosyncratically, say, with the preposition *on*.

(257) a. John sang (about Mary/ *on Mary).
  b. John zang (on Mary).

Furthermore, the locution *Mandela is talking on freedom tonight* (contrast *Our gospel group is singing on freedom*) marks the theme with *on* instead of *about*. We predict, correctly, that this special use of *talk* for 'to give a talk on' has an obligatory theme (i.e. the topic of the talk).

This prediction follows from the present account because semantically optional roles are not specified within individual lexical entries, but instead are subject only to general pragmatic and semantic conditions.

---

important differences: (i) the GB principle does not prohibit c-selection for optional roles. E.g., it would not rule out the hypothetical verb *zang* in (257). (ii) The GB principle is an axiom, while (255) is a deduction.

2 The Semantics of Argument Structure Revisited

In Chapter 2 I give some rather strong constraints on argument structure. These are stated as conditions on the ordering of roles which must apply whenever certain lexical entailments obtain. Take the Notion-Rule for example (51):

(258) The Notion-Rule.

A lexical sign meeting this description is ill-formed:

$$* \begin{bmatrix} \text{REL} & R \\ \text{ROLES} & <...[\text{ROLE1}]...[\text{ROLE2}]...> \end{bmatrix},$$

if the following lexical entailment holds:
$$\forall x, y \,\square\, [R \,(\text{ROLE1}:y, \text{ROLE2}:x) \rightarrow CONCEIVE(x,y)]$$

It forbids any lexical entry whose content includes a relation and role list such that the relation involves the filler of the lower slot *CONCEIVE*-ing of the filler of the higher slot.

But this rule is probably too strong. Exceptions like *concern* and *preoccupy* are mentioned above (Chapter 2, section 1.3), where it is noted that verbs of this kind are relatively rare. Still, no account is actually offered for them. Where a few exceptions appear, more are sure to be found. Tony Davis (forthcoming) notes that the verb *elude* may also counterexemplify the Notion Rule:

(259) The proof of the Goldbach conjecture has so far eluded
      mathematicians.

This sentence seems to entail that the mathematicians have had a notion of the proof of the Goldbach conjecture; indeed any sentence of the form 'x eluded y' entails that y has a notion of x, so this verb violates the Notion Rule. More generally, the status of exceptions within the theory needs to be addressed squarely.

We begin by recasting the lexical entailments in different terms. Consider the entailments which drives the Notion-Rule for verbs *like, see,* and *believe* respectively. These state that all liking, seeing, or believing (of y by x) involves conceiving (of y by x), or:

(260) $\forall x,y[\textbf{\textit{LIKE}}$ (LIKER:x, LIKEE:y) $\rightarrow CONCEIVE(x,y)]$

  $\forall x,y[\textbf{\textit{SEE}}$ (SEER:x, SEEN:y) $\rightarrow CONCEIVE(x,y)]$

  $\forall x,y[\textbf{\textit{BELIEVE}}$ (BELIEVER:x, BELIEVED:y) $\rightarrow CONCEIVE(x,y)]$

Instead we will capture these constraints by positing that the relations *like, see*, and *believe* are subsorts of the relation *conceive*:

(261) Sortal hierarchy of relations (world knowledge)

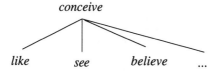

Like the necessary constraints, this sortal hierarchy captures world knowledge. Roughly speaking (but see presently), the fact that the *like* relation is a subsort of the *conceive* relation means that any psoa satisfying description (262a) must also satisfy the more general (less informative) description (262b):

(262) a.

$$\begin{bmatrix} \text{REL} & \textit{like} \\ \text{LIKER} & [\ ] \\ \text{LIKEE} & [\ ] \end{bmatrix}$$

b.

$$\begin{bmatrix} \text{REL} & \textit{conceive} \\ \text{CONCEIVER} & [\ ] \\ \text{CONCEIVED} & [\ ] \end{bmatrix}$$

Since any psoa of the former type is also of the latter type, then the entailments given above follow automatically.

Actually, simply specifying that the *like* relation is a subsort of the *conceive* relation is not quite sufficient to capture our intuitive knowledge of the relation between liking and conceiving. In addition we know that the liker argument corresponds to the conceiver and the likee to the conceived and not vice versa; e.g. *John liked the beans* entails that John had a notion of the beans, but not that the beans had a notion of John. There are two possible ways to add this information. One way is to posit a higher order matching condition in which attributes names are sorted, so that LIKER is a subsort of CONCEIVER and LIKED is a subsort of CONCEIVED (see Pollard and Sag 1994:342). A simpler alternative which we adopt here is to relabel the argument roles of the *like* relation, so the former LIKER is now called CONCEIVER and the former LIKEE is now called CONCEIVED. (This is modelled on the approach to the lexicosemantics of control proposed in Pollard and Sag 1994:285ff.) Hence we rewrite (262a) above as:

$$
\begin{bmatrix}
\text{REL} & like \\
\text{CONCEIVER} & [\ ] \\
\text{CONCEIVED} & [\ ]
\end{bmatrix}
$$

Now it is clear that—

$$
\begin{bmatrix}
\text{REL} & conceive \\
\text{CONCEIVER} & [\ ] \\
\text{CONCEIVED} & [\ ]
\end{bmatrix}
\quad \text{subsumes} \quad
\begin{bmatrix}
\text{REL} & like \\
\text{CONCEIVER} & [\ ] \\
\text{CONCEIVED} & [\ ]
\end{bmatrix}
$$

— as desired.

Next we need to introduce an ordering into our roles. Departing from the proposal in Chapter 2 above, we leave the roles unordered within the psoa, and instead add a list-valued feature ROLES. The ROLES items are ordered by a small set of basic *predicate sorts*, one to replace each of the argument selection rules. (Cp. the *predicator structures* of Davis 1993, forthcoming). The predicate sorts partition the sort *predicate*, which is a subsort of *synsem*. (Roughly speaking, *synsem* objects of the sort *predicate* are those with a SUBJ list; see section 3 below.)

(263) Sortal hierarchy of predicates (universal grammar).

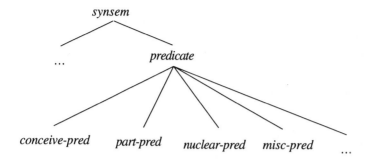

These predicate sorts capture the argument ordering information of the corresponding rules. For example, let us replace the Notion-Rule with the following sort declaration *conceive-pred* predicate sort:

(264) Sort declaration for *conceive-pred*.

$$conceive\text{-}pred: \begin{bmatrix} \text{ROLES} & < [\ ]_{[1]}, [\ ]_{[2]} > \\ \text{CONTENT} & \begin{bmatrix} \text{REL} & conceive \\ \text{CONCEIVER} & [1] \\ \text{CONCEIVED} & [2] \end{bmatrix} \end{bmatrix}$$

All verbs to which the Notion-Rule applied non-vacuously to yield the argument ordering will now, by stipulation, be of the sort *conceive-pred*. An example is the verb *like*. The lexical entries for *like, see,* and *believe* are approximately as follows:

(265) Lexical sign for *like*:

$$\begin{bmatrix} conceive \text{-} pred \\ \text{ROLES} & < \text{NP}, \text{NP} > \\ \text{CONTENT} & [\text{REL } like] \end{bmatrix}$$

(266) Lexical sign for *see*:

$$\begin{bmatrix} conceive \text{-} pred \\ \text{ROLES} \quad <\text{NP, NP}> \\ \text{CONTENT} \begin{bmatrix} \text{REL} & see \end{bmatrix} \end{bmatrix}$$

(267) Lexical sign for *believe*:

$$\begin{bmatrix} conceive \text{-} pred \\ \text{ROLES} \quad <\text{NP, NP}> \\ \text{CONTENT} \begin{bmatrix} \text{REL} & believe \end{bmatrix} \end{bmatrix}$$

When we spell out the information from the sort declaration (264), we arrive at this fuller lexical sign for *like*:

(268) Lexical sign for *like*, with *conceive-pred* information spelled out:

$$\begin{bmatrix} conceive \text{-} pred \\ \text{ROLES} \qquad <\text{NP}_{[1]}, \text{NP}_{[2]}> \\ \text{CONTENT} \begin{bmatrix} \text{REL} & like \\ \text{CONCEIVER} & [1] \\ \text{CONCEIVED} & [2] \end{bmatrix} \end{bmatrix}$$

Section 3 below explores in detail the interpretation of the ROLES ordering, but for now we can simplify by looking at it as if it were the SUBCAT list: the first (leftmost) NP corresponds to the subject and the second NP is the object. Thus the above lexical sign represents the desired result: the 'conceiver' (liker) role is assigned to the subject and the 'conceived' (likee) role is assigned to the object.

Crucially, only a verb whose REL value successfully unifies with *conceive* can be of the sort *conceive-pred*. As a consequence, a language learner will never be tempted to misclassify the verbs *please* or *frighten* as a *conceive-pred*, since these verbs do not necessarily involve the experiencer conceiving of the theme, as demonstrated in Chapter 2.

Thus, for a verb to be a *conceive-pred*, its relation must be a subsort of the *conceive* relation. Notice that this is a necessary but not a sufficient condition. This makes possible a more satisfactory treatment of lexical exceptions than is possible on the argument selection theory in Chapter 2.

For example, while I argue that many of the 'Theme-Subject, Experiencer-Object' verbs like *please* are only apparent exceptions, as the conceive relation is not actually entailed, there are some genuine exceptions such as *concern* and *preoccupy*, as shown by the contradictory nature of the sentences in (71), repeated here:

(269) a. #Toxic waste concerns the Senator deeply— he just happens to be unaware of its existence.

b. #The most recent massacre of defenseless people by the U.S. military was so brutal that it preoccupies even those who do not know that it occurred.

c. *John is trying hard to concern/preoccupy Mary, but she couldn't care less about him.

Indeed, there may be other exceptions. On our revised version, we assume that the *concern* and *preoccupy* relations are subsorts of the *conceive* relation, but that the *synsem* values of the verbs *concern* and *preoccupy* are not of the sort *conceive-pred*.

We could go further and note that the set of exceptional verbs form a semantic subparadigm: *concern* and *preoccupy* both involve a mental state in which the experiencer is necessarily rather strongly affected, in contrast with milder states such as stative *please* or *bother*. If this generalization is valid and can be made precise then this would indicate the presence of a new predicate sort (say, *stative-affect-pred*), to be added to the hierarchy in (263) above. If not then such verbs could be thrown into a catch-all *miscellaneous-pred* sort. This would include both exceptional verbs, which semantically fit another sort but have the unexpected list order, and unclassifiable verbs, which fit none of the sorts. An example of the latter might be the verb *comprise*, as in *The U.S. comprises 50 states*. Generally one would assume that the set of predicate sorts is fairly small and universal. To the extent that more than one classification for a lexical item is possible, languages vary somewhat in the classification of such 'miscellaneous' lexical items.

It is worth noting that erroneous reverse linking for transitives— e.g. *Beans hate me* for *I hate beans*— is strikingly absent from the otherwise rich array of linking errors observed in the speech of children and adults. For example, false causatives like *I almost fell you down* and *That decided me* are common among children and adults alike (data from Pinker 1989:323, 154). But when the wrong argument is selected as subject of a verb, the argument which should have been the subject is not moved to the object but rather to an oblique, as in the attested *Can germs harbor in these things?* (from Pinker 1989:155)— rather than the unattested *Can germs *harbor these things?* Similarly, in her study of the acquisition of Korean case-marking, Chung (1994) found that even during the stage when children made many nominative and accusative case-marking errors of various types, conspicuously absent are any errors in which nominative-object accusative-subject incorrectly replaces the nominative-subject accusative-object linking.

The few exceptions that I am aware of for adult English speakers occur among the 'semantically syncategorematic' verbs, i.e those which fit none of the predicate sorts. For instance reverse linking with *comprise*, as in **Fifty states comprise the Union.*, is a common violation of the prescriptive usage rule, which favors *The Union comprises fifty states*, although this 'error' is becoming increasingly accepted (only 61% of the 1976 American Heritage Dictionary usage panel rejected the first sentence).

In contrast to the paucity of argument ordering errors among children, preposition selection errors are common. As in other lexical acquisition, children overextend the use of a form to cover too broad a range of meanings. The particular semantic directions of this overextension reveal a lot about human conceptual categories, as argued by Clark and Carpenter (1989), inter alia. They observe that children often incorrectly use *from* to mark agents and causes, as in errors such as *These fall down from me, He isn't going to get hurt from those bad guys* (*from* replacing *by*), and *From I put it under here* (*from* replacing *because*). Clark and Carpenter argue persuasively, on the basis of acquisition by children and data from other languages and earlier forms of English, for a so-called 'emergent category' of SOURCE which comprises locative sources, agents, causes, etc. This category reflects an underlying universal conceptual notion. Children extend the locative *from* into the nonlocative domain of the emergent category until they eventually learn the correct forms: 'Children's emergent categories may fit some conventions of some languages from the start. Where this is not the case, as for agents and causes in English, children must replace earlier nonconventional uses with conventional ones.' (Clark and Carpenter 1989:25)

Assuming this conclusion about the notion SOURCE is correct, it provides evidence for what might be called coarse-grained thematic role types which apply across semantic domains. It also suggests that such thematic role types (if that is what we choose to call them) can be seen as the basis for a theory of polysemy: because of the underlying conceptual notion SOURCE, locative sources, agents, causes, etc. will tend to cluster together as meanings for a given form— though of course this is only a rough guide to actual adult grammars (after all, the examples of children's speech are errors). But this result clearly does not militate in favor of the view that these thematic role types are relevant to linking theory, except indirectly, in the sense that linking and polysemy are both concerned with lexical meaning. Instead, I believe that the universal conceptual notions underlying roles list ordering are even more abstract and coarse-grained than, e.g., SOURCE, and instead involve relations like *conceive*, *part-whole*, and so on.

3 Valence and subjects

Next we need to reconsider how the ordering of roles will have its effect in the syntax. In the previous chapters we posited a mapping between items of the ROLES and the SUBCAT list, subject to the Isomorphy Principle, which states that the mapping of unrestricted roles must be an order isomorphism. Let us consider incorporating an idea from more recent work in HPSG by replacing the SUBCAT list with two distinct 'valence' lists, a SUBJ list for the subject (if any) and a COMPS list for any (non-subject) complements (Borsley 1987, Pollard and Sag 1994, Chapter 9). This revised picture involves three lists:

$$
\begin{bmatrix}
\text{SUBJ} & <...> \\
\text{COMPS} & <...> \\
\text{ROLES} & <...> \\
\text{CONTENT} & [\ ]
\end{bmatrix}
$$

The SUBJ and COMPS lists each takes a list value; the value of SUBJ is a list of length zero or one, while the COMPS list is of any length. Some arguments for this revision are summarized in Pollard and Sag 1994, Chapter 9.

The old Subcategorization Principle, which had the effect of cancelling items from the SUBCAT list as phrases are concatenated with the head, is generalized to the Valence Principle, which acts on the SUBJ and COMPS lists (Pollard and Sag 1994:348):

(270) Valence Principle
    In a headed phrase, for each valence feature F, the F value of the head daughter is the concatenation of the phrase's F value with the list of SYNSEM values of the F-DTRS value. (where F ranges over SUBJ and COMPS)

The list we call ROLES corresponds roughly to a list called SUBCAT or ARG-S (mnemonic for 'argument structure') in other work within this revised model. We retain the term ROLES for consistency with previous chapters of this book. The old mapping between the ROLES and SUBCAT lists is now replaced with a mapping between the ROLES list and the valence lists SUBJ and COMPS. The status of these features depends on which syntactic or semantic processes are defined on each list, which is an open issue. Here we assume minimally that:

(i) the ROLES list is the locus of lexicosemantic generalizations about argument structure, as enforced by argument selection rules such as the Notion-Rule, or the Predicate Sorts which replace them (see section 2 above); and

(ii) the valence lists (SUBJ and COMPS) are the locus of phrase structure concatenation, as enforced by the Valence Principle.

For the moment we can leave open just which list(s) are the proper site for defining other processes such as binding and control (see below regarding control).

Take the verb *chases* for example:

$$
\begin{bmatrix}
\text{SUBJ} & <[1]\text{NP}[nom]_{[3sg]} > \\
\text{COMPS} & <[2]\text{NP} > \\
\text{ROLES} & <[1]_{[3]},[2]_{[4]} > \\
\text{CONTENT} & \begin{bmatrix} \text{REL} & \text{chase} \\ \text{CHASER} & [3] \\ \text{QUARRY} & [4] \end{bmatrix}
\end{bmatrix}
$$

Unlike SUBJ and COMPS, ROLES is not a valence feature, hence not subject to the Valence Principle, so the ROLES list items are not cancelled off as complements are added. Omitting the CONTENT features for simplicity, the sentence *Fido chases Felix* would have the following structure:

(271)

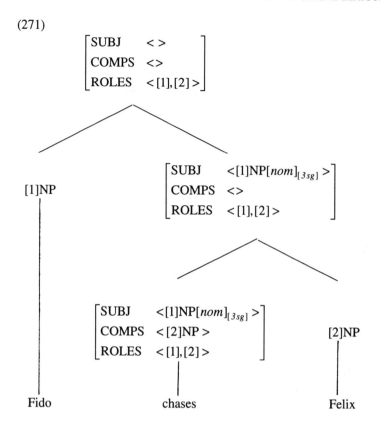

Now let us consider linking, that is, the mapping between the ROLES list and the valence lists.

Which role maps to the subject? With the verb *chase*, the 'highest' (=left-most) ROLES list item maps to the SUBJ list, and the remaining role maps to the COMPS list. Indeed, it is generally the rule that the highest ROLES list item is the subject— *as long as that item is an appropriate syntactic category to be a subject*. English subjects generally must be NP's or (*marked*, i.e. complementizer-introduced) clauses like *That it is raining pleases me greatly*, and not PP's or other categories.[6] We capture this fact with the following sort declaration for English predicates:

---

[6]Under analyses which treat locative PP's in the locative inversion construction (*Under the bed was an old can of paint*) as subjects (e.g. Bresnan and Kanerva 1989), we would need to allow such PP subjects as well. We ignore this possibility for simplicity.

(272) Sort declaration for *predicate* (English)

    predicate: [SUBJ < NP ∨ S[*marked*] >]

What if the highest ROLES list item is a PP and hence not a possible subject? Consider for example some verbs of possession such as *own*, *possess*, and *have*, as well as verbs of transfer of possession such as *receive*, *buy*, and *borrow*:

(273) a.   Fred owns this book.
      b.   Fred possesses this book.
      c.   Fred has this book.
      d.   Fred received/bought/borrowed/etc. this book.

With all of these verbs the possessor argument is the subject and the possession is the object. Suppose we posit a new predicate sort *possess-pred* to capture this generalization:

(274) Sort declaration for *possess-pred*:

$$
\begin{bmatrix}
\text{ROLES} & < [\ ]_{[1]}, [\ ]_{[2]} > \\
\text{CONTENT} & \begin{bmatrix} \text{REL} & possess \\ \text{POSSESSOR} & [1] \\ \text{POSSESSION} & [2] \end{bmatrix}
\end{bmatrix}
$$

As in the previous section, we assume that the relations denoted by *have*, *own*, etc. are all subsorts of the *possess* relation (part of world knowledge), and that each of these verbs is lexically designated as a *possess-pred* (part of linguistic knowledge). In light of this pattern, consider the verb *belong:*

(275) a.   *Fred belongs this book.
      b.   *This book belongs Fred.
      c.   *To Fred belongs this book.
      d.   This book belongs to Fred.

Is *belong* an exception to the pattern of other verbs of possession? Understood properly, it is not exceptional. Suppose *belong*, like the other verbs, is a *possess-pred*, but it happens that its possessor argument is lexically specified as a PP[*to*] (where the preposition *to* is, perhaps, selected according to the account in section 1 above).

(276) Lexical sign for the verb *belong*.

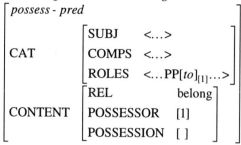

$$\begin{bmatrix} possess\text{-}pred \\ CAT \quad \begin{bmatrix} SUBJ & <...> \\ COMPS & <...> \\ ROLES & <...PP[to]_{[1]}...> \end{bmatrix} \\ CONTENT \quad \begin{bmatrix} REL & belong \\ POSSESSOR & [1] \\ POSSESSION & [\ ] \end{bmatrix} \end{bmatrix}$$

Spelling out the information from the sort declarations of *possess-pred* and its supersort *predicate*, we get:

$$\begin{bmatrix} possess\text{-}pred \\ CAT \quad \begin{bmatrix} SUBJ & <NP> \\ COMPS & <...> \\ ROLES & <PP[to]_{[1]},[\ ]_{[2]}> \end{bmatrix} \\ CONTENT \quad \begin{bmatrix} REL & belong \\ POSSESSOR & [1] \\ POSSESSION & [2] \end{bmatrix} \end{bmatrix}$$

Now, what about the mapping from the ROLES list to the valence lists? Let us hypothesize that quite generally the subject maps onto the highest (=leftmost) 'syntactically possible' role. The highest syntactically possible role is [ ]$_{[2]}$ in this instance, since PPs cannot be subjects in English. So we state our linking principle as follows:[7]

(277) Linking Principle (universal)
   a. The SUBJ list item is token-identical with the highest allowable ROLES list item.
   b. The COMPS list contains any remaining ROLES list items.

Applying this linking principle to the lexical sign for *belong*, we get:

---

[7]Clause (277b) of the Linking Principle is clearly too vague. I am ignoring the issue of the ordering of the COMPS list items relative to the corresponding ROLES list items, as this would take us too far afield. This issue does not arise in the examples below because the COMPS list has only one member.

$$
\begin{bmatrix}
\textit{possess - pred} \\[4pt]
\text{CAT} \quad
\begin{bmatrix}
\text{SUBJ} & <[4]\text{NP}> \\
\text{COMPS} & <[3]> \\
\text{ROLES} & <[3]\text{PP}[to]_{[1]},[4]_{[2]}>
\end{bmatrix} \\[18pt]
\text{CONTENT} \quad
\begin{bmatrix}
\text{REL} & \text{belong} \\
\text{POSSESSOR} & [1] \\
\text{POSSESSION} & [2]
\end{bmatrix}
\end{bmatrix}
$$

This is the correct result: in *This book belongs to Fred*, the possession argument maps to the subject, while the possessor is a complement PP[*to*].

As a second example, consider the verb *appear* in the sense 'be visible' or 'become visible.' The theme (i.e. that which is visible) is expressed as the subject, and the experiencer (i.e. the agent to whom the theme is visible) is normally unexpressed and understood as the speaker or the point-of-view of the discourse (278a). The experiencer can sometimes be expressed as a PP[*to*], especially in descriptions of private experiences such as dreams and visions:

(278) a. Suddenly a car appeared (?to us) on the horizon.
　　　 b. Xochipilli appeared to him (in a vision).
　　　 c. *He appeared Xochipilli.
　　　 d. *To him appeared Xochipilli.

The *appear* relation is a subsort of the *conceive* relation, since the experiencer must have a visual notion of the theme (see Chapter 2 above). Suppose this verb is an ordinary *conceive-pred* (i.e. that it is not an exception of the sort discussed in section 2 above). Then the experiencer (= conceiver) precedes the theme (= conceived) in the ROLES list. But the experiencer role happens to be lexically marked as a PP:

(279) Lexical sign for *appear*

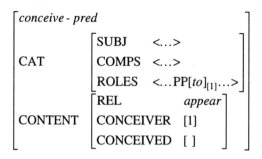

$$
\begin{bmatrix}
conceive\text{-}pred \\
\text{CAT} \quad
\begin{bmatrix}
\text{SUBJ} & <...> \\
\text{COMPS} & <...> \\
\text{ROLES} & <...PP[to]_{[1]}...>
\end{bmatrix} \\
\text{CONTENT} \quad
\begin{bmatrix}
\text{REL} & appear \\
\text{CONCEIVER} & [1] \\
\text{CONCEIVED} & [\ ]
\end{bmatrix}
\end{bmatrix}
$$

As above, we spell out the information from the *conceive-pred* sort declaration, and also the information from the predicate sort declaration (since *conceive-pred* is a subsort of *predicate*):

$$
\begin{bmatrix}
conceive\text{-}pred \\
\text{CAT} \quad
\begin{bmatrix}
\text{SUBJ} & < NP > \\
\text{COMPS} & <...> \\
\text{ROLES} & < PP[to]_{[1]},[\ ]_{[2]} >
\end{bmatrix} \\
\text{CONTENT} \quad
\begin{bmatrix}
\text{REL} & appear \\
\text{CONCEIVER} & [1] \\
\text{CONCEIVED} & [2]
\end{bmatrix}
\end{bmatrix}
$$

Now consider linking. As in the previous example, the highest ROLES item, [1]PP[*to*], is not a possible subject since it is not an NP. Therefore the highest *possible* ROLES item is [2]. By the Linking Principle above, this item is structure-shared with the SUBJ list item and the remaining role enters the COMPS list:

$$
\begin{bmatrix}
conceive\text{-}pred \\
\text{CAT} \quad
\begin{bmatrix}
\text{SUBJ} & < [4]NP > \\
\text{COMPS} & < [3] > \\
\text{ROLES} & < [3]PP[to]_{[1]},[4]_{[2]} >
\end{bmatrix} \\
\text{CONTENT} \quad
\begin{bmatrix}
\text{REL} & appear \\
\text{CONCEIVER} & [1] \\
\text{CONCEIVED} & [2]
\end{bmatrix}
\end{bmatrix}
$$

This model also handles the passive voice very straightforwardly, without an operation on lists (as in Pollard and Sag 1987) or a system of proto-arguments added solely to handle the passive (as in Kathol 1994). On the present account, a passive verb is simply a verb which, like active *belong* and *appear* in the previous examples, has a highest role that is syntactically inappropriate to be a subject. In the case of the passive, the highest role is inappropriate as a subject either because it is expressed as a PP[*by*] or because it is not expressed at all, as in (280b):

(280) a.   The students like James.
       b.   James is liked (by the students).

Following is the lexical entry for the verb *like*, with information from the *conceive-pred* (and *predicate*) sort declarations indicated.

(281) Lexical entry for the verb stem *like*.

$$
\begin{bmatrix}
\textit{conceive - pred} \\
\text{CAT} \quad
\begin{bmatrix}
\text{SUBJ} & <\text{NP}> \\
\text{COMPS} & <...> \\
\text{ROLES} & <[\ ]_{[1]}, \text{NP}_{[2]}> \\
\end{bmatrix} \\
\text{CONTENT} \quad
\begin{bmatrix}
\text{REL} & \text{like} \\
\text{CONCEIVER} & [1] \\
\text{CONCEIVED} & [2] \\
\end{bmatrix}
\end{bmatrix}
$$

Following is the information encoded in the passive morphology. For simplicity we consider only the variant with the *by*-phrase.

(282) Information accompanying the passive (with by-phrase)

$$
\begin{bmatrix}
\textit{passive - verb} \\
\text{CAT} \quad
\begin{bmatrix}
\text{HEAD} & \textit{verb}[\text{VFORM } \textit{passive}] \\
\text{ROLES} & < \text{PP}[\textit{by}],...> \\
\end{bmatrix}
\end{bmatrix}
$$

Since the preposition *by*-phrases impose no thematic restrictions (cp. non-agentive *by*-phrases as in *The vowel is preceded by a consonant*), we assume that the *by*-phrase is [–r]. When we unify in the passive information we arrive at the following:

(283) Lexical entry for the passive verb *liked* (before linking).

$$
\begin{bmatrix}
conceive\text{-}pred \\[4pt]
\text{CAT} \quad
\begin{bmatrix}
\text{SUBJ} & <\text{NP}> \\
\text{COMPS} & <...> \\
\text{ROLES} & <\text{PP}[by]_{[1]}, \text{NP}_{[2]}>
\end{bmatrix} \\[4pt]
\text{CONTENT} \quad
\begin{bmatrix}
\text{REL} & like \\
\text{CONCEIVER} & [1] \\
\text{CONCEIVED} & [2]
\end{bmatrix}
\end{bmatrix}
$$

After adding the information from the Linking Principle (277) to (281) and (283), we arrive at (284) for the active verb and (285) for the passive verb, respectively.

(284) Lexical entry for the active verb *like* after linking.

$$
\begin{bmatrix}
conceive\text{-}pred \\[4pt]
\text{CAT} \quad
\begin{bmatrix}
\text{SUBJ} & <[3]> \\
\text{COMPS} & <[4]> \\
\text{ROLES} & <[3]\text{NP}_{[1]}, [4]\text{NP}_{[2]}>
\end{bmatrix} \\[4pt]
\text{CONTENT} \quad
\begin{bmatrix}
\text{REL} & like \\
\text{CONCEIVER} & [1] \\
\text{CONCEIVED} & [2]
\end{bmatrix}
\end{bmatrix}
$$

(285) Lexical entry for the passive verb *liked* after linking.

$$
\begin{bmatrix}
conceive\text{-}pred \\[4pt]
\text{CAT} \quad
\begin{bmatrix}
\text{SUBJ} & <[4]\text{NP}> \\
\text{COMPS} & <[3]> \\
\text{ROLES} & <[3]\text{PP}[by]_{[1]}, [4]\text{NP}_{[2]}>
\end{bmatrix} \\[4pt]
\text{CONTENT} \quad
\begin{bmatrix}
\text{REL} & like \\
\text{CONCEIVER} & [1] \\
\text{CONCEIVED} & [2]
\end{bmatrix}
\end{bmatrix}
$$

Since PP[by]$_{[1]}$ is not an NP, it is not eligible to be a subject. Hence the highest allowable role for the subject is NP$_{[2]}$.

Even more interesting consequences of this theory are found when we apply it to cross-linguistic comparisons. Languages vary parametrically according to what categories they allow as subjects. By relativizing our Linking Principle ((277) above) to categorial conditions on subjects, we can immediately explain many cross-linguistic variations in linking patterns. Take the problem of subject selection with German and Icelandic dative experiencer verbs like Icelandic *líka* and German *gefallen*, both meaning 'like' (or 'please').

(286) Mér   líka   eir bílar.   (Icelandic)
       me-Dat   like   those cars-Nom
       'I like those cars.'

(287) Mir   gefallen   diese Damen.   (German)
       me-Dat   please   these-Nom ladies
       'I like these ladies.'

The two verbs have similar if not equivalent meaning, and they have the same case marking pattern: dative experiencer and nominative theme. But this superficial similarity masks an important difference: in the Icelandic sentence the dative experiencer is the subject, while in the German sentence the nominative theme is the subject, as demonstrated thoroughly by Andrews (1976), Cole et al (1980), and Zaenen et al (1985), inter alia. Among the evidence for this, German dative experiencers cannot be controllees (288), while Icelandic dative experiencers can ((288) is from Cole et al 1980:727; ex. (289) is from Harbert and Toribio 1991:131):

(288) a.   *Ich versuchte,   diese Damen   zu gefallen.   (G.)
         I   tried   these-Nom ladies   to please
         ('I tried to like these ladies.')

      b.   Diese Damen$_i$ versuchten,   PRO$_i$ mir   zu gefallen.
         these ladies   tried   me-Dat   to please
         'These ladies tried to please (= be liked by) me.'

(289) Ég$_i$ vonast   til að   PRO$_i$ líka   þessir bílar.   (Ic.)
       I   hope   to   like   those cars
       'I hope to like those cars.'

Also, in German it is the nominative theme but in Icelandic the dative experiencer (if anything), which controls a 'without'-clause or 'instead of'-clause (from Harbert and Toribio 1991:170, ex. 33):

(290) German

    a.   weil   mir   das Mädchen$_i$ gefiel,   anstatt   PRO$_i$
        because me-D   the-N girl   pleased   instead.of

        mich   zu überwältigen
        me   to overpower
        'because the girl pleased me instead of PRO overpowering me.'

    b.   *weil   mir$_i$ das Mädchen gefiel,   ohne   PRO$_i$
        because me-D   the girl   pleased, without

        es   zu wollen
        it   to want
        'because I$_i$ liked the girl, without PRO$_i$ wanting to.'

(291) Icelandic

    a.   *af því að   méer   líkaði   stéulkan$_i$ í stað þess   að
        because   me-D   liked   girl-the   instead of   to
        PRO$_i$ þreyta   mig
                 tire   me
        'because the girl pleased me, instead of PRO tiring me.'

    b.   ?af því að   méer$_i$ léikaði   stéulkan   áan þess   að
        because   me-D   liked   girl-the   without   to
        PRO$_i$ vilja   það
                 want   it
        'because I$_i$ liked the girl without PRO$_i$ wanting to.'

As you can see from these examples, the German verb (in 290) and the Icelandic verb (in 291) have opposite preferences for the controller of the adjunct clause. This too supports the view that the nominative theme is the German subject, but the dative experiencer the Icelandic subject, since generally objects cannot control such clauses.

    Where in the grammar is this difference between German and Icelandic located? Under the present assumptions the difference between the behavior of the verbs in the two languages reduces to a very simple difference in the syntax of the two languages: German has a condition that its subjects must be nominative, while Icelandic lacks this condition.

In Icelandic we find subjects of each of the cases— nominative, accusative, dative, and genitive— as illustrated in the following examples, respectively. Each example is accompanied by a raising construction to show that the NP in question is truly the subject (data from Andrews 1982):

(292) a. Hann   elskar   hana.   *Nominative subject*
         he-N   loves   her-A
         'He loves her.'

      b. Hann   virðist   elska   hana.
         he-N   seems   to.love   her-A
         'He seems to love her.'

(293) a. Hana   vantar   mat.   *Accusative subject*
         her-A   lacks   food-A
         'She lacks food.'

      b. Hana   virðist   vanta   mat.
         her-A   seems   lack.inf   food-A
         'She seems to lack food.'

(294) a. Barninu   batnaði   veikin.   *Dative subject*
         the.child-D recovered.from   the.disease-N
         'The child recovered from the disease.'

      b. Barninu   virðist   hafa   batnað   veikin.
         the.child-D seems   have.inf recovered-from the.disease-N
         'The child seems to have recovered from the disease.'

(295) a. Verkjanna   gætir   ekki.   *Genitive subject*
         the.pains-G   is.noticeable   not
         'The pains are not noticeable.'

      b. Verkjanna   virðist   ekki   gæta.
         the.pains-G   seems   not   be.noticeable.inf
         'The pains don't seem to be noticeable.'

Non-nominative NPs in German, while superficially similar to the Icelandic subjects, fail all subject tests. As noted above, they cannot be controllees ('PRO') or 'arbitrary PRO' (data from Zaenen et al. 1985):

(296) a.   Mir   ist   übel.
        me-D is   nasty
        'I am nauseated.'

     b.   *Mir hofft/*Ich hoffe   übel   zu sein.   *dative PRO*
        me-D hopes/I-N hope   nauseated to be
        ('I hope to be nauseated.')

     c.   *Übel   zu sein ist unangenehm.   *dative PRO$_{arb}$*
        nauseated to be   is   disagreeable
        ('To be nauseated is disagreeable.')

By way of contrast, nominative NPs can of course be controlled or arbitrary PRO (data from Zaenen et al. 1985):

(297) a.   Im Sommer zu reisen ist   angenehm.   *nominative PRO$_{arb}$*
        in summer   to travel is   agreeable
        'To travel in summer is nice.'

     b.   Er   hofft   weg   zu gehen.   *nominative PRO*
        he   hopes   away to go
        'He hopes to go away.'

This contrasting behavior can even be seen in cognate verb pairs such as the passive forms of *helfen* (German) and *hjálpa* (Icelandic) 'help'.

(298) a.   Honum   var   hjálpað.   (Icelandic)
        him-D   was   helped

     b.   Ihm   wurde geholfen.   (German)
        him-D was   helped
        'He was helped.'

The dative argument of Icelandic 'help' can be a controllee, at least in some dialects—

(299) a. %ₒEg vonast til að verða hjáalpað.
I   hope   for to be   helped.

'I hope to be helped.'

b. Að vera   hjálpað í prófinu   er óleyfilegt.
to be   helped   on the-exam   is disallowed

'To be helped on the exam is not allowed.'

—while the dative argument of German 'help' cannot (data from Zaenen et al 1985):

(300) a. *Wir möchten von der Polizei geholfen werden.
we   wish   by the police   helped   AUX
('We wished to be helped by the police.')

b. *Geholfen zu werden ist angenehm.
helped   to be   is   agreeable
('To be helped is nice.')

Further subjecthood tests confirming the conclusion that Icelandic, but not German, has non-nominative subjects, include relative clause reduction, reflexivization, and subject ellipsis. See Andrews 1976 and 1982, Thráinsson 1979, Cole et al 1980, and Zaenen et al 1985 for discussion.

To capture this phenomenon in our framework we will make the single list item in the value of SUBJ be our formalization of the notion 'subject' as used above. This means, for example, that a controlled VP such as *[PRO mir zu gefallen]* in (288b) has a single item on its SUBJ list (which is coindexed with its controller) and an empty COMPS list. To put it imprecisely, a controllee subject (or 'PRO') must be the SUBJ. This move is not strictly necessary but it is a reasonable view, since it treats controlled VPs (e.g. non-finite VPs) like finite VPs.[8]

---

[8]Notice that in example (290a) the subject *das Mädchen* intervenes between the verb and its dative object, suggesting that the clause has a flat structure: i.e. the HEAD-SUBJECT-COMPLEMENT Schema of Pollard and Sag 1994:388. Word order in the German 'middle field' is subject to many factors besides grammatical relations, including relative 'thematic

This distinction between German and Icelandic can be encoded with different sort declarations for predicates in the two languages.

(301) *predicate:* [SUBJ < (NP[*nom*]) >]   (German)

(302) *predicate:* [SUBJ < (NP) >]   (Icelandic)

The NP[*nom*] is optional because clauses do not require subjects; e.g. (296a) above has no subject. A subjectless sentence arises whenever there is no 'highest allowable ROLES item', i.e. when no ROLES item is a possible subject. The German sort declaration states that a German verb or other predicate has either a nominative NP subject or no subject at all. Notice, incidently, that this nominative case condition for German applies even if the subject is a controllee, hence not syntactically expressed. Indeed, Henniss (1989) has persuasively argued from coordination facts of Malayalam that the so-called PRO subject (i.e. the unrealized controlled subject) must receive case even though that case is not realized morphologically.

By way of illustration, let us consider linking for the German and Icelandic verbs for 'like'. Following is the lexical sign for either Icelandic *líka* or German *gefallen*, where [*obl*] is a case value which is a supersort of the oblique cases (dative, genitive):

(303) Lexical sign for German *gefallen* or Icelandic *líka*:

$$
\begin{bmatrix}
\textit{conceive - pred} \\[4pt]
\text{CAT} \quad
\begin{bmatrix}
\text{SUBJ} & <...> \\
\text{COMPS} & <...> \\
\text{ROLES} & <..[1]\text{NP}[obl]...>
\end{bmatrix} \\[14pt]
\text{CONTENT} \quad
\begin{bmatrix}
\text{REL} & \textit{like} \\
\text{CONCEIVER} & [1] \\
\text{CONCEIVED} & [2]
\end{bmatrix}
\end{bmatrix}
$$

---

prominence' (see Uszkoreit 1987) which for us corresponds roughly to ROLES list order. Indeed, complement order in these examples would be explained by the hypothesis that unmarked word order follows the ROLES list order.

Since dative is the regular case of experiencers, the oblique case gets specified as dative by the general process described in section 1 above. (Of course the distribution of dative may differ in minor ways across the two languages.) Adding this information plus the information in the sort declaration for *conceive-pred*, we derive the following lexical sign for the German and the Icelandic verb:

(304) Lexical sign for German *gefallen* or Icelandic *líka*:

$$
\begin{bmatrix}
conceive\text{-}pred \\[4pt]
\text{CAT} \quad
\begin{bmatrix}
\text{SUBJ} & <...> \\
\text{COMPS} & <...> \\
\text{ROLES} & <[1]\text{NP}[dat],[2]\text{NP}>
\end{bmatrix} \\[4pt]
\text{CONTENT} \quad
\begin{bmatrix}
\text{REL} & like \\
\text{CONCEIVER} & [1] \\
\text{CONCEIVED} & [2]
\end{bmatrix}
\end{bmatrix}
$$

Since *conceive-pred* is a subsort of *predicate*, we add the information from the sort declaration for *predicate* (see (301) and (302) above). Since the sort declarations for the two languages differ, we arrive at two different lexical signs:

(305) Icelandic *líka*:

$$
\begin{bmatrix}
conceive\text{-}pred \\[4pt]
\text{CAT} \quad
\begin{bmatrix}
\text{SUBJ} & <\text{NP}> \\
\text{COMPS} & <...> \\
\text{ROLES} & <\text{NP}[dat]_{[1]},\text{NP}_{[2]}>
\end{bmatrix} \\[4pt]
\text{CONTENT} \quad
\begin{bmatrix}
\text{REL} & like \\
\text{CONCEIVER} & [1] \\
\text{CONCEIVED} & [2]
\end{bmatrix}
\end{bmatrix}
$$

(306) German *gefallen*:

$$
\begin{bmatrix}
\textit{conceive - pred} \\[4pt]
\text{CAT} \quad
\begin{bmatrix}
\text{SUBJ} & <\text{NP}[\textit{nom}]> \\
\text{COMPS} & <...> \\
\text{ROLES} & <\text{NP}[\textit{dat}]_{[1]}, \text{NP}_{[2]}>
\end{bmatrix} \\[6pt]
\text{CONTENT} \quad
\begin{bmatrix}
\text{REL} & \textit{like} \\
\text{CONCEIVER} & [1] \\
\text{CONCEIVED} & [2]
\end{bmatrix}
\end{bmatrix}
$$

This predicts different linking patterns in the two languages for otherwise similar verbs. Recall the Linking Principle (277), repeated here:

(307) Linking Principle (universal)
    a. The SUBJ list item is token-identical with the highest allowable ROLES item.
    b. The COMPS list contains any remaining ROLES items.

For the Icelandic verb the highest allowable ROLES item is the dative experiencer; for the German verb the dative experiencer is not allowable, so the highest allowable ROLES item is the theme. Applying the universal linking rules to the two lexical signs gives the following:

(308) Icelandic *líka*:

$$
\begin{bmatrix}
\textit{conceive - pred} \\[4pt]
\text{CAT} \quad
\begin{bmatrix}
\text{SUBJ} & <[3]> \\
\text{COMPS} & <[4]> \\
\text{ROLES} & <[3]\text{NP}[\textit{dat}]_{[1]}, [4]\text{NP}_{[2]}>
\end{bmatrix} \\[6pt]
\text{CONTENT} \quad
\begin{bmatrix}
\text{REL} & \textit{like} \\
\text{CONCEIVER} & [1] \\
\text{CONCEIVED} & [2]
\end{bmatrix}
\end{bmatrix}
$$

(309) German *gefallen*:

$$
\begin{bmatrix}
\textit{conceive - pred} \\[2pt]
\text{CAT}\quad
\begin{bmatrix}
\text{SUBJ} & <[4]\text{NP}[\textit{nom}]> \\
\text{COMPS} & <[3]> \\
\text{ROLES} & <[3]\text{NP}[\textit{dat}]_{[1]},[4]\text{NP}_{[2]}>
\end{bmatrix} \\[6pt]
\text{CONTENT}\quad
\begin{bmatrix}
\text{REL} & \textit{like} \\
\text{CONCEIVER} & [1] \\
\text{CONCEIVED} & [2]
\end{bmatrix}
\end{bmatrix}
$$

This is the correct result: subject tests pick out the dative experiencer for Icelandic but the theme for German, as shown above. The two words have virtually the same 'thematic structure', i.e. the same meaning; they even have the same dative experiencer case marking pattern. But the languages differ in their categorial conditions on subjects, and so by relativizing our linking principle to those conditions we are able to explain the differences in attested linking patterns.

This analysis captures a central insight of Kiparsky 1987, namely that the mapping between thematic roles and grammatical relations depends upon parochial morphosyntactic properties of the language (indeed the present account owes a great deal to Kiparsky's proposals). In Kiparsky's theory the morphosyntactic 'resources' of the language, such as case features, are called *linkers*. He defends the so-called 'direct linking' view, where thematic roles map directly onto these morphosyntactic features and grammatical relations such as subject and object are defined on linked structures.

This theory also explains the behavior of the 'covert datives' of Dutch and Swedish discussed in Chapter 3 above. Recall that Dutch 'datives', that is, non-nominative experiencers and recipients which correspond to the German datives, cannot be subjects, as illustrated by example (226), repeated here:

(310) a.   Jan   hoopt   Marie   te   bevallen.
           Jan   hopes   Marie   to   please.inf
           'John hopes to please Mary.'
           (not: 'John hopes that Mary will please him.'

b. Hem bevallen is niet moeilijk.
   him please.inf is not difficult
   'To please him is not difficult.'
   (not: 'To be pleased by him is not difficult.')

The controlled subject of the bracketed VPs is the theme, not the experiencer, as indicated by the glosses. To account for this we need only assume that Dutch has the German type of sort declaration for *predicate*:

(311) *predicate:*   [SUBJ < (NP[*nom*]) >]

Dutch verbs like *bevallen* 'like' may be assumed to have the same lexical sign as the German and Icelandic verbs given in (304) above. In particular, *bevallen* lexically assigns non-nominative case to the experiencer, which therefore cannot be expressed as the subject. Since Dutch does not morphologically distinguish dative from accusative, we might wish to replace the [*dat*] feature with [*acc*]; but in other relevant respects the Dutch verb is identical to that of Icelandic and German, and Dutch syntax is like German in having a nominative subject requirement.

4 Summary

This chapter's revised model can be summarized as follows (compare diagram (234) in Chapter 3):

(312) Summary of conditions on the lexical signs of predicators

		type of condition	*representation*
SUBJ	< ... >	conditions on	language-specific sort
COMPS	< ... ... >	SUBJ values	declaration for *predicate*
	⇑ ⇑	mapping between lists	universal Linking
	linking	relative to list orders	Principle
	⇓ ⇓	& conditions on SUBJ	
ROLES	< ... ... >	lexicosemantics of	universal sort
CONTENT	[...]	ROLES list order	declarations for
			subsorts of *predicate*

Several revisions have been suggested in this chapter:

(i) *Preposition selection.* We altered the rules for combining verbs with the PPs they govern. In this way, the semantic conditions on preposition selection previously captured by the Restricted Linking Principle, will instead fall out from general rules of compositional semantics.

(ii) *Argument ordering.* The ROLES list order can be captured by specifying an order for each of several *predicate* sorts (where *predicate* is a subsort of *synsem*). A sortal hierarchy of psoa descriptions ensures that only verbs with appropriate CONTENT values can have a *synsem* value belonging to a particular *predicate* sort. This sortal hierarchy effectively replaces the lexical entailments with relations between psoa descriptions: e.g. every actual psoa described by a 'liking psoa' description is also described by a 'conceiving psoa' description. This revised model is arguably more elegant, and also allows us to capture subparadigms of exceptions and idiosyncratic lexical exceptions.

(iii) *Valence lists.* Language-wide morphosyntactic conditions on subjects can influence the linking between roles and complements. We account for this by relativizing our principles for mapping from roles to complements, to the categorial possibilities specified for subjects by the language in question.

References

Åfarli, Tor A. 1989a. Passive in Norwegian and in English. *Linguistic Inquiry*, 20.1, 101-108.

Åfarli, Tor A. 1989b. *The Syntax of Norwegian Passive Constructions.* University of Trondheim Working Papers in Linguistics 9 (Doctor Artium thesis, Dept. of Linguistics, University of Trondheim.)

Åkermalm, Åke. 1961. Fast Sammansättning och Lös Förbindelse. *Nysvenska Studier*, 41, 175-196.

Alsina, Alex and Sam A. Mchombo. 1993. Object Asymmetries and the Chichewa Applicative Construction. In Sam A. Mchombo, ed., *Theoretical Aspects of Bantu Grammar*, 17-45. Stanford, Calif.: CSLI Publications.

Andrews, Avery. 1976. The VP complement in Modern Icelandic. *Montreal Working Papers in Linguistics* 6, 1-22.

Andrews, Avery. 1982. The Representation of Case in Modern Icelandic. In Joan Bresnan, ed., 1982, 427-503.

Anward, Jan. 1981. Functions of Passive and Impersonal Constructions—A Case Study from Swedish. Doctoral dissertation, Department of Linguistics, Uppsala University.

Baker, C. L. 1968. *Indirect Questions in English.* Doctoral dissertation, University of Illinois, Urbana.

Baker, Mark C. 1988. *Incorporation— A Theory of Grammatical Function Changing.* Chicago: University of Chicago Press.

Barwise, Jon and John Perry. 1983. *Situations and Attitudes.* Cambridge, Mass.: MIT Press.

Bierwisch, Manfred. 1988. Thematic Grids as Interface Between Syntax and Semantics. Colloquium talk, Stanford University Linguistics Department.

Borsley, Robert. 1987. Subjects and Complements in HPSG. Technical report no. CSLI-107-87. Stanford, Calif.: CSLI Publications.

Bresnan, Joan. 1982. Control and Complementation. In Joan Bresnan, ed., 1982, 283-390.

Bresnan, Joan, ed. 1982. *The Mental Representation of Grammatical Relations.* Cambridge, Mass.: MIT Press.

Bresnan, Joan and Annie Zaenen. 1990. Deep Unaccusativity in LFG. In Katarzyna Dziwirek, Patrick Farrell, and Errapel Mejías-Bikandi, eds.,

Grammatical Relations: A Cross-Theoretical Perspective, 45-57. Stanford, Calif.: Stanford Linguistics Association and CSLI Publications.

Bresnan, Joan and Jonni Kanerva. 1989. Locative Inversion in Chichewa: A Case Study of Factorization in Grammar. *Linguistic Inquiry* 20.1., 1-50.

Bresnan, Joan and Lioba Moshi. 1990. Object Asymmetries in Comparative Bantu Syntax. *Linguistic Inquiry* 21.2, 147-185.

Carlson, Greg and Thomas Roeper. 1980. Morphology and Subcategorization: Case and the Unmarked Complex Verb. In Teun Hoekstra, Harry van der Hulst, and Michael Moortgat, eds., *Lexical Grammar*. Dordrecht: Foris.

Chomsky, Noam. 1981. *Lectures on Government and Binding*. Dordrecht: Foris.

Chomsky, Noam. 1986. *Barriers*. Cambridge, Mass.: MIT Press.

Chung, Gyeonghee. 1994. *Case and Its Acquisition in Korean*. Doctoral Dissertation, University of Texas Linguistics Department, Austin, Texas.

Clark, Eve and Kathie Carpenter. 1989. The Notion of Source in Language Acquisition. *Language* 65.1, 1-30.

Cole, Peter, Wayne Harbert, Gabriella Hermon, and S. N. Sridhar. 1980. The Acquisition of Subjecthood. *Language* 56.4, 719-743.

Condoravdi, Cleo. 1989. The Middle: Where Semantics and Morphology Meet. *MIT Working Papers in Linguistics*, vol. 12. Cambridge, Mass.

Craig, Colette and Kenneth Hale. 1988. Relational preverbs in some languages of the Americas: typological and historical perspectives. *Language* 64.2, 312-344.

Crimmins, Mark. 1989. *Talk About Beliefs*. Doctoral dissertation, Stanford University Philosophy Department.

Crimmins, Mark and John Perry. 1989. The Prince and the Phone Booth: Reporting Puzzling Beliefs. *The Journal of Philosophy,* vol. 86, no. 12, 685-711.

Croft, William. 1991. *Syntactic Categories and Grammatical Relations: The Cognitive Organization of Information*. Chicago: University of Chicago Press.

Davidson, Donald. 1967. The Logical Form of Action Sentences. In Nicholas Rescher, ed., *The Logic of Decision and Action.* Pittsburgh: University of Pittsburgh Press, 115-120.

Davis, Tony. 1993. Linking, Inheritance, and Semantic Structures. Handout for Stanford Linguistics Department Colloquium, April 16, 1993.

Davis, Tony. Forthcoming. Linking and Lexical Semantics in the Hierarchical Lexicon. Doctoral Dissertation, Stanford University.

den Besten, Hans. 1985. The Ergative Hypthesis and Free Word Order in Dutch and German. In Jindrich Toman, ed., *Studies in German Grammar*, 23-100. Dordrecht: Foris.

Devlin, Keith 1991. *Logic and Information.* Cambridge: Cambridge University Press.

Di Sciullo, Anna-Maria and Edwin Williams. 1987. *On the Definition of Word.* Cambridge, Mass.: MIT Press.

Dowty, David. 1972. On the Syntax and Semantics of the Atomic Predicate CAUSE. *Proceedings of the Chicago Linguistic Society* 8, 62-74.

Dowty, David. 1979. *Word Meaning and Montague Grammar.* Dordrecht: Reidel.

Dowty, David. 1986. On the Semantic Content of the Notion Thematic Role. In Gennaro Chierchia, Barbara Partee and Ray Turner, eds., *Property Theory, Type Theory and Natural Language Semantics.* Dordrecht: Reidel.

Dowty, David. 1991. Thematic Proto-Roles and Argument Selection. *Language* 67.3, 547-619.

Dowty, David, Robert Wall and Stanley Peters. 1981. *Introduction to Montague Semantics.* Dordrecht: Reidel.

Ejerhed, Eva. 1983. Swedish Verb-Particle Constructions: Syntactic and Semantic Problems. Unpublished manuscript, Umeå, Sweden.

Emonds, Joseph E. 1976. *A Transformational Approach to English Syntax: Root, Structure-Preserving, and Local Transformations.* New York: Academic Press.

Fillmore, Charles. 1965. *Indirect Object Constructions in English and the Ordering of Transformations.* London: Mouton & Co.

Fillmore, Charles. 1968. The Case for Case. In Emmon Bach and Robert T. Harms, eds., *Universals in Linguistic Theory.* New York: Holt, Rinehart, Winston.

Flickinger, Daniel. 1987. *Lexical Rules in the Hierarchical Lexicon.* Doctoral dissertation, Stanford University Linguistics Department.

Foley, William A. and Robert Van Valin. 1984. *Functional Syntax and Universal Grammar.* Cambridge: Cambridge University Press.

Gawron, Jean Mark. 1986. Situations and Prepositions. *Linguistics and Philosophy* 9, 327-382.

Goldberg, Adele. 1992. The Inherent Semantics of Argument Structure: The Case of the English Ditransitive Construction. *Cognitive Linguistics* 3.1, 37-74.

Green, Georgia. 1974. *Semantics and Syntactic Regularity.* Indiana University Press, Bloomington.

Grimshaw, Jane. 1990. *Argument Structure.* MIT Press, Cambridge, MA.

Gropen, Jess, Steven Pinker, Michelle Hollander, Richard Goldberg, and Ronald Wilson. 1989. The Learnability and Acquisition of the Dative Alternation in English. *Language* 65:2, 203-257.

Gruber, Jeffrey S. 1976. *Lexical Structures in Syntax and Semantics.* North-Holland Linguistic Series no. 25. Amsterdam: North-Holland Publishing Co.

Hankamer, Jorge and Ivan Sag. 1976. Deep and Surface Anaphora. *Linguistic Inquiry* 7.3, 391-428.

Harbert, Wayne and Almeida Toribio. 1991. Nominative Objects. In Almeida Toribio and Wayne Harbert, eds., *Cornell Working Papers in Linguistics no. 9,* 127-192. Department of Modern Languages and Linguistics, Cornell University.

Henniss, Kathryn. 1989. 'Covert' Subjects and Determinate Case: Evidence from Malayalam. In Jane E. Fee and Katherine Hunt, eds., *Proceedings of the Eighth West Coast Conference on Formal Linguistics,* 167-175. Stanford, Calif.: CSLI Publications.

Hinrichs, Erhard. 1985. A Compositional Semantics for Aktionsarten and NP Reference in English. Doctoral dissertation, Ohio State University.

Huddleston, Rodney. 1984. *Introduction to the Grammar of English.* Cambridge University Press.

Hume, David. 1968/1888. *A Treatise of Human Nature.* Lewis A. Selby-Bigge, ed. Oxford: Oxford University Press.

Jackendoff, Ray. 1972. *Semantic Interpretation in Generative Grammar.* MIT Press, Cambridge, MA.

Jackendoff, Ray. 1976. Towards an Explanatory Semantic Representation. *Linguistic Inquiry* 7:1, 89.

Jackendoff, Ray. 1983. *Semantics and Cognition.* MIT Press, Cambridge, MA.

Jackendoff, Ray. 1987. The Status of Thematic Relations in Linguistic Theory. *Linguistic Inquiry* 18:3, 369-411.

Jackendoff, Ray. 1990. *Semantic Structures.* MIT Press, Cambridge, MA.

Johnston, Michael. 1992. The Syntax and Semantics of Purposive Adjuncts in English. Doctoral qualifying paper, Department of Linguistics, University of California at Santa Cruz.

Kathol, Andreas. 1994. Passives Without Lexical Rules. In John Nerbonne, Klaus Netter, and Carl Pollard, eds., *German in Head-Driven Phrase Structure Grammar*, 237-272. Stanford, Calif.: CSLI Publications.

Kiparsky, Paul. 1987. *Morphology and Grammatical Relations.* Manuscript, Stanford University.

Kiparsky, Paul. 1988. Agreement and Linking Theory. Manuscript, Stanford University.

Krifka, Manfred. 1987. *Nominal Reference and Temporal Constitution: Towards a Semantics of Quantity.* Forschungsstelle für Natürlich-sprachliche Systeme, Universität Tübingen.

Ladusaw, Bill and David Dowty. 1987. Towards a Nongrammatical Account of Thematic Roles. In Wendy Wilkins, ed., *Syntax and Semantics 21: Thematic Relations,* 61-73. New York: Academic Press.

Levin, Lori. 1987. *Toward a Linking Theory of Relation Changing Rules in LFG.* CSLI Report Number CSLI-87-115. Stanford, Calif.: CSLI Publications.

Lewis, David. 1973. Causation. *The Journal of Philosophy* 70, 556-567.

Link, Godehard. 1983. The Logical Analysis of Plurals and Mass Terms: A Lattice-Theoretical Approach. In Rainer Bauerle, Christoph Schwarze, and Arnim von Stechow, eds., *Meaning, Use, and Interpretation of Language,* 302-323. Berlin: de Gruyter.

Marantz, Alec P. 1984. *On the Nature of Grammatical Relations.* Linguistic Inquiry Monograph 10. Cambridge, Mass.: MIT Press.

Mithun, Marianne. 1984. The Evolution of Noun Incoporation. *Language* 60, 847-93.

Moravcsik, Julius. 1990. *Thought and Language.* Routledge, London.

Nunberg, Geoffrey, Ivan Sag, and Thomas Wasow. 1994. Idioms. *Language* 70.3, 491-538.

Oehrle, Richard T. 1976. *The Grammatical Status of the English Dative Alternation.* Doctoral dissertation, Massachusetts Institute of Technology.

Ostler, Nicholas. 1979. *Case-Linking: a Theory of Case and Verb Diathesis Applied to Classical Sanskrit.* Doctoral dissertation, Massachusetts Institute of Technology.

Pesetsky, David. 1987. Binding Problems with Experiencer Verbs. *Linguistic Inquiry* 18, 126-140.

Pinker, Steven. 1989. *Learnability and Cognition—The Acquisition of Argument Structure*. Cambridge: MIT Press.

Pollard, Carl and Ivan Sag. 1987. *Information-Based Syntax and Semantics— Vol. 1 Fundamentals*. Stanford: CSLI Publications.

Pollard, Carl and Ivan Sag. 1992. Anaphors in English and the Scope of Binding Theory. *Linguistic Inquiry* 23.2, 261-303.

Pollard, Carl and Ivan Sag. 1994. *Head-Driven Phrase Structure Grammar*. Stanford, Calif.: CSLI Publications; and Chicago: University of Chicago Press.

Roeper, Thomas. 1981. On the Deductive Model and the Acquisition of Productive Morphology. In C. L. Baker and John J. McCarthy, eds., *The Logical Problem of Language Acquisition*, 129-164. Cambridge: MIT Press.

Sag, Ivan A. 1985. Grammatical Hierarchy and Linear Precedence. CSLI Report No. 60, Stanford, Calif.: CSLI Publications.

Searle, John R. 1984. *Intentionality—An Essay in the Philosophy of Mind*. Cambridge: Cambridge University Press.

Shieber, Stuart 1986. *An Introduction to Unification-Based Approaches to Grammar*. CSLI Lecture Notes 4, Stanford: CSLI Publications.

Shopen, Timothy, ed. 1985. *Language Typology and Syntactic Description. Vol. III.: Grammatical Categories and the Lexicon*. Cambridge: Cambridge University Press.

Smith, Henry. 1992. *Restrictiveness in Case Theory*. Doctoral dissertation, Department of Germanic Studies, Stanford University.

Talmy, Leonard. 1985. Lexicalization Patterns: Semantic Structure in Lexical Forms. In Timothy Shopen ed., 1985, 57-149.

Tan, Fu. 1991. *Subjecthood in Chinese*. Doctoral dissertation, Stanford University Linguistics Department.

Tenny, Carol. 1987. *Grammaticalizing Aspect and Affectedness*. Doctoral dissertation, Massachusetts Institute of Technology.

Thráinsson, Höskuldur. 1979. *On Complementation in Icelandic*. New York: Garland Publishing.

Uszkoreit, Hans. 1987. *Word Order and Constituent Structure in German*. Stanford: CSLI Publications.

Van Valin, Robert. 1990. Linking Theory in Role and Reference Grammar. Stanford University Linguistics Department Colloquium, Stanford.

Vendler, Zeno. 1967. *Linguistics in Philosophy.* Ithaca, NY: Cornell University Press.

Wechsler, Stephen. 1989. Accomplishments and the Verbal Prefix *re-*. *Proceedings of the Northeastern Linguistic Society XIX.*

Wechsler, Stephen. 1991. A Non-Derivational Account of the English Benefactive Alternation. Paper read at the 65th meeting of the Linguistic Society of America, Chicago.

Wechsler, Stephen. 1994. Preposition Selection Outside the Lexicon. To appear in *Proceedings of the Thirteenth West Coast Conference on Formal Linguistics.*

Wechsler, Stephen and Yae-Sheik Lee. To appear. The Domain of Direct Case Assignment. To appear in *Natural Language and Linguistic Theory.*

Wellander, Erik. 1973. *Riktig Svenska.* Stockholm: Esselte Studium.

Williams, Edwin. 1981. Argument Structure and Morphology. *Linguistic Review* 1, 81-114.

Zaenen, Annie. 1987. The Syntax of Bevallen ('please'). Presentation at the Center for the Study of Language and Information, Stanford.

Zaenen, Annie 1993. Unaccusativity in Dutch: Integrating Syntax and Lexical Semantics. In James Pustejovsky, ed., *Semantics and the Lexicon,* 129-162. Dordrecht: Kluwer Academic Publishers.

Zaenen, Annie, Joan Maling, and Höskuldur Thráinsson. 1985. Case and Grammatical Functions: the Icelandic Passive. *Natural Language and Linguistic Theory* 3, 441-483.

Other titles in the Dissertations in Linguistics Series

Theoretical Aspects of Kashaya Phonology and Morphology
Eugene Buckley

This study discusses a wide range of phonological and morphological phenomena in Kashaya, a Pomoan language of northern California, and considers their implications for current theories of generative grammar. The volume raises issues in feature theory, presents prosodic analysis, and discusses numerous morphological patterns.

420 p. ISBN: 1-881526-03-8 (cloth); ISBN: 1-881526-02-X (paper)

The Structure of Complex Predicates in Urdu
Miriam Butt

This volume takes a detailed look at two differing complex predicates in the South Asian language Urdu. The Urdu permissive in particular brings into focus the problem of syntax-semantics mismatch. Urdu shows that argument structure must be considered independent of syntactic structures, but be related to grammatical relations via a theory of linking. This work counters that the recent move towards increasingly abstract argument structure representations do not allow an adequate characterization of the case marking patterns, and that semantic factors such as volitionality must play a role in linking.

257 p. ISBN: 1-881526-59-3 (cloth); ISBN: 0-937073-58-5 (paper)

On the Placement and Morphology of Clitics
Aaron Halpern

Using data from a variety of languages, this book investigates the place clitics in the theory of language structure, and their implications for the relationships between syntax, morphology, and phonology. It is argued that the least powerful theory of language requires us to recognize at least two classes of clitics, one with the syntax of independent phrases and the other with the syntax of inflectional affixes. These classes may be diagnosed on the basis of both distributional and morphological differences although there is considerable overlap.

260 p. ISBN: 1-881526-48-8 (cloth); ISBN: 1-881526-47-X (paper)

Configuring Topic and Focus in Russian
Tracy Holloway King

This work examines word order and the encoding of topic and focus in Russian. As has long been observed, word order in Russian encodes specific discourse information: with neutral intonation, topics precede discourse-neutral constituents which precede foci. The author extends this idea to show that word order encodes different types of topic and focus in a principled manner. The interaction of topic and focus with the syntax and the nature of phrase structure in general has been vigorously debated in recent linguistic literature. This work's in-depth analysis of Russian elucidates this debate since Russian contains both configurational and non-configurational characteristics.

271 p. (est.) ISBN: 1-881526-63-1 (cloth); ISBN: 1-881526-62-3 (paper)

Phrase Structure and Grammatical Relations in Tagalog
Paul Kroeger

This volume examines the history of the subjecthood debate in the syntax of Philippine languages. Using data from Tagalog, the assertion is made that grammatical relations such as subject and object are syntactic notions, and must be identified on the basis of syntactic properties, rather than by semantic roles or discourse functions. The conclusions drawn entail consequences for many approaches to syntax including the Government-Binding theory.

240 p. ISBN: 0-937073-87-3 (cloth); ISBN: 0-937073-86-5 (paper)

Argument Structure in Hindi
Tara Mohanan

Arguing for a conception of linguistic organization, this book involves the factorization of syntactically relevant information into at least four parallel dimensions of structure: semantic structure, argument structure, grammatical function structure, and gram-matical category structure. The author argues that these dimensions are co-present, being simultaneously accessible for the statement of regularities.

285 p. ISBN: 1-881526-44-5 (cloth); ISBN: 1-881526-43-7 (paper)

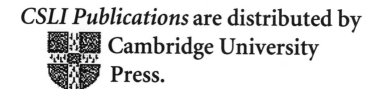

CSLI Publications are distributed by Cambridge University Press.